SEACOAST FORTIFICATIONS
OF THE UNITED STATES:
An Introductory History

Emanuel Raymond Lewis

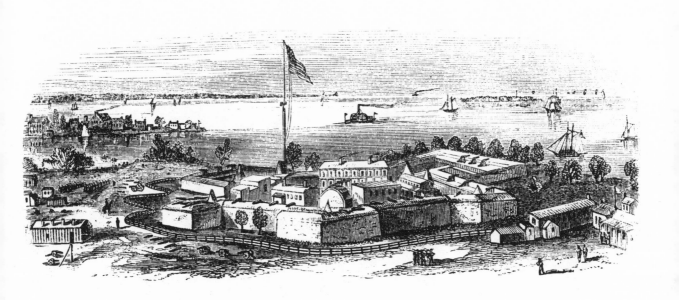

PRESIDIO

To Clarence Edward Cotter
Colonel, United States Army, Retired

When this book appeared in 1970, it was the first publicly available work in nearly a century on the subject of harbor defense fortification and seacoast artillery in the United States; it was also the only book to carry the subject into the twentieth century and to its conclusion following World War II. It revived interest in a long-forgotten element of military preparedness which had been very near the core of our national defense philosophy throughout most of our history.

It is not surprising, therefore, that in the few years since its publication *Seacoast Fortifications of the United States* strongly influenced historical preservation activities in this country and the literature of American military history. In 1970 Dr. Lewis wrote of the relatively few efforts to restore or even preserve remnants of our coastal defenses. Since then such efforts have increased enormously, in many instances due to the direct or indirect influence of this book. Rarely has a single work reawakened such interest in a particular field or instilled this interest, for the first time, in a whole new generation of readers, many of whom had never before heard of seacoast defenses.

At the time of initial publication by the Smithsonian Institution, the book's subject matter was regarded as esoteric or at least highly specialized. Certainly the need for a large printing was unanticipated. Even before the first printing was exhausted, however, the interest generated by the book had spread beyond anyone's expectations. And within a few years, enthusiasts as well as scholars of military history, architecture, and technology could not obtain copies. Thus the decision to republish was both welcome and necessary. No revision was needed, but a few corrections have been made and some things brought up to date. For all practical purposes this is the original, already a classic in the field.

James L. Collins, Jr.
Brigadier General, USA
Chief of Military History

CONTENTS

PREFACE TO THE FIRST PRINTING

During most of this nation's history, security against foreign attack was sought largely through defense of its maritime frontiers. The two principal instruments of this security were the Navy and the seacoast fortifications of the Army.

The Navy's coastal defense role has been abundantly documented elsewhere and is remarked upon only briefly in these pages. The Army's activities in this aspect of defense, on the other hand, have been almost totally neglected in both historical and technical literature, despite the fact that the fortifying of harbors in this country was carried out almost continuously for a century and a half and was an important and at times a central element in American military policy. To be sure, there exists a small, fragmentary literature consisting of pamphlets or articles pertaining to individual forts, but for every fort thus described, dozens remain ignored. More important, no previous attempt has been made to deal with these works in systematic terms. As a result, there is no unifying literature to pull the whole together, to indicate that such fortifications were, in fact, elements of cohesive systems, or even to suggest that the efforts devoted to this type of defense in the United States proceeded in a number of distinct steps or generations, each exhibiting a particular architectural style and representing a particular level of weaponry development.

The reasons for this neglect are not entirely clear. Perhaps it has stemmed from the fact that the occasions on which coastal forts were actually engaged in combat were few and infrequent. More likely, it has been due to the fact that the large majority of American military structures prior to World War II were modest, rapidly built frontier forts neither standard in design nor permanent in character. Hundreds of such works were constructed to protect inland positions and lines of communication, generally by soldiers or civilians, untrained in military engineering, who used whatever materials happened to be at hand. Unlike the forts of mainland Europe, which were huge, permanent, and highly systematized defensive works erected to protect cities and guard land frontiers—and about which, incidentally, there is a substantial literature—the forts of the American interior, although often of considerable historical importance, were for the most part of little technical or architectural significance.

In the United States, only on the seacoasts in the vicinity of harbor entrances to the great cities and important naval bases were large permanent defensive works constructed. It was toward these points, where the possibility of attack by well-armed naval forces had to be faced, that the principal engineering talents of the Army were directed. To the extent that this nation has an enduring heritage of military architecture, it is to be found along the coasts, in the vicinity of some of our most populous and important cities.

It is not proposed in this work to examine in any depth the origins, the conduct, or the wisdom of the policies that led to the extensive fortification of our seaports, though some of these questions are raised briefly at the outset. Rather, this work surveys the products of these policies, with an emphasis on the development of their architecture and their armament. Basically, it deals with the characteristics of the several generations of defensive works, and with the interrelationships of fortification design and the nature of weapon technology at various periods. The examples used to illustrate the defenses of each generation have, so far as possible, been selected from among specimens still in existence, particularly from among those which have undergone a minimum of structural change since their original planning and construction.

For the benefit of the general reader every effort has been made to avoid or as necessary to clarify technical terminology and the classical vocabulary of fortification. Because of the brevity of this work, its emphasis is upon the salient features of the various generations of defenses and on their defining marks, rather than upon superficial detail. By such emphasis it seeks to achieve a concise yet systematic presentation of this important aspect of the American military and architectural heritage.

Many persons have contributed directly to the growth of this work from its beginning as a brief paper presented early in 1966 before the Pacific Northwest History Conference at Portland, Oregon. The continued encouragement of John A. Hussey, Western Regional Historian, National Park Service, who was present and first urged the extension and publication of the paper, has been of great help at every stage.

For their valuable advice on many aspects of the research and writing,

I should like to thank Victor Gondos, Jr., former Chief, Army and Navy Branch, National Archives; Harold L. Peterson, Chief Curator, National Park Service; and Commander David P. Kirchner, U.S. Navy, longtime collaborator on studies of seacoast fortification.

Thanks are due also to James S. Hutchins, Assistant Director of the Smithsonian Institution's National Armed Forces Museum Advisory Board, who steered the manuscript through several rounds of reviews, and to its Director, Colonel John H. Magruder III.

Among the many individuals who gave generously of their time in order to read various revisions of the text and to offer constructive criticism were: Edwin Bearss, Division of History, National Park Service; Martin Blumenson, Washington, D.C.; Judge Charles S. Crookham, Portland, Oregon; Professor Philip A. Crowl, The University of Nebraska; Marshall Hanft, Oregon State Archives; Robert W. Krauskopf, Director, Modern Military Records Division, National Archives; Philip K. Lundeberg, National Museum of History and Technology, Smithsonian Institution; Professor Preston Onstad, Oregon State University; Jesse A. Remington, Chief, Historical Section, Office of the Chief of Engineers, Department of the Army; Donald L. Sichel, Corvallis, Oregon; Richard K. Smith, National Air and Space Museum, Smithsonian Institution; and Professor Russell F. Weigley, Temple University.

There are several persons without whose help this work could not have been prepared. The documentary research was made possible and aided significantly by Herbert A. Gale, George Goldfine, and Marie Phipps, all of San Francisco, California; Sara Jackson and Jessie Midkiff, both of the National Archives and Records Service, Washington, D.C.; and Hannah Zeidlik, Office, Chief of Military History, Washington. Studies in the field were assisted immeasurably, sometimes at risk of limb, by Eleanor Lewis, Joan Bush, Lois Kirchner, and Edward DeLanis, who carried maps, plans, notebooks, and cameras on what must, at times, have been exhausting forays into military archeology.

The illustrations in this work have been drawn from a variety of sources, including public collections, federal agencies, private organizations, and individuals. For their assistance and generosity in providing photographs, I should like to thank the Audiovisual Branch of the National Archives, the Still [pictures] Depository of the U.S. Air Force, the U.S. Army Photographic Agency, the U.S. Naval Photographic Center, and the National Park Service, Department of the Interior. Various other Army and Navy offices, as well as other organizations and individuals, have granted permission to use illustrative materials in their possession. These are credited in the individual captions, along with the available data on dates and original sources. The geographical locations at which illustrations originated are keyed in Appendix A.

The drawing on page 73, copyright 1941 by W. W. Norton & Company, Inc. (renewed 1968 by James E. Hicks), is reproduced by permission of the publisher.

Finally, I wish to express my especial gratitude to Stetson Conn, Chief Historian, Department of the Army, who has never hesitated to render every assistance and encouragement, not only to the preparation of this particular work, but to many other efforts as well.

E. R. L.

July 1969

PREFACE TO THE SECOND PRINTING

In presenting this work again, nearly a decade after its first appearance, certain changes were viewed as necessary, others as desirable. Subsequent to the initial publication in 1970, a few errors—very few, fortunately—were discovered in the original version. More commonly, events during the intervening years had rendered certain material, particularly some of the figure captions, no longer accurate. In one or two cases, readers had pointed out an ambiguity in text or caption.

As it is intended to present this work in a form as close to the original as possible, yet with the desire to rectify the flaws noted above, we—the publishers and I—have adopted a sort of compromise position: to change within the text and figure captions only that material that was, to begin with, in error; and to indicate here, in this special preface, those changes that need to be made as a consequence of events since the first printing.

The genuine errors occurred in a few of the illustrations, such as the line maps of Figure 1, where some localities were wrongly placed and a few were omitted. There were also a couple of errors in captions, such as those for Figures 15 and 18, in both of which 10-inch guns were incorrectly identified as 15-inch.

Changes stemming from events over the last several years should be noted as follows:

The final sentences of the captions to both Figures 9 and 11 should be read to include the fact that Governors Island is now [1979] the headquarters of the U.S. Coast Guard's Atlantic Area and Third District.

In the final sentence of the caption to Figure 21, delete "Continental Army Command (CONARC)," and substitute therefor "Army Training and Doctrine Command (TRADOC)."

In the final sentence of the caption to Figure 23, delete "New York State Maritime Academy," and substitute therefor "State University of New York, Maritime College."

In the last complete sentence on page 129, the first word, "Hundreds," should now read "Dozens."

In view of what promises to be a continually changing situation, the final paragraph of the text (on page 134) should begin: "The National Park Service administers *many* areas. . . ."

A few readers were troubled by a wording in the caption to Figure 56, feeling that the phrase "installed between 1921 and 1924" suggested that the guns remained in place for that brief period only. In fact, it took that long to install them, and they were not removed until after World War II.

Turning to less practical matters, I'd like to make a couple of comments of a personal nature. The years since the initial appearance of this work have been marked not only by the sorts of events calling for the changes noted above, but also by a human toll. Several of the individuals mentioned in the preface to the original printing are gone, among them Harold L. Peterson, who wrote the book's postscript. Pete's passing, on New Year's day of 1978, was a great personal loss to many of us, and a great professional loss to many, many others throughout the world.

I wish to thank General James L. Collins, Jr., the Army's Chief of Military History, for the very kind words of introduction he has provided for this new printing.

And, finally, I must express my singular gratitude to Crimilda Pontes, Designer to the Smithsonian Institution. For various reasons, her extraordinary talent and her role in the production of this book went unacknowledged in the original printing. A gifted artist and a lovely person, she gave to this work what is best about it. Mine were only the ideas, the words, and the pictures—she is the one who put it all together and gave it life.

E. R. L.

May, 1979

BACKGROUND:

Historical and Technical Rationale

The Defense Tradition

Early in 1794 the United States, as a new nation, undertook its first program of defensive construction for the protection of its seacoast communities against naval attack. This was the first of a series of harbor defense programs that were to continue, virtually without interruption, until shortly after World War II. The large and varied body of coastal fortifications resulting from this century and a half of construction constituted this country's principal expression of military architecture during most of that period.

These defenses had far more than architectural significance, however, for the fortifications, as well as the history of legislation that produced them, accurately typified certain basic characteristics of this nation's traditional responses to threats from abroad. Not only did they represent the distinctly defensive emphasis of its military and naval policies throughout most of the nineteenth century and much of the twentieth; to a large degree they also symbolized the general attitudes of Americans, public and Congress alike, toward the entire question of national defense.[1]

In the entire history of warfare, few principles have been as durable or as nearly absolute as the one concerning the superiority of guns ashore over guns afloat. Accordingly, for several hundred years the permanent emplacement of heavy artillery to defend cities and naval bases on or near the sea was an almost universal practice among maritime nations, for the mere presence of such defenses ordinarily constituted a highly reliable deterrent to naval attack.[2] Only after World War II and the appearance of radically new forms of weaponry such as nuclear explosives and guided missiles did the major powers finally abandon the use of conventional coast artillery, though many smaller countries have to the present day retained this inexpensive yet effective means of guarding critical coastal localities.

For a unique combination of geographical, historical, and traditional reasons, seacoast fortification represented a peculiarly attractive means of defense in the United States, where at times it was carried on to an extent

1. The existing literature on harbor defense fortifications, what there is of it, is almost entirely technical. The only contemporary works to give the subject more than passing mention with regard to its place in American defense policy are Walter Millis, *Arms and Men* (New York: G. P. Putnam's Sons, 1956); and Russell F. Weigley, *Towards an American Army* (New York: Columbia University Press, 1962), chapters 5 and 9.
2. The rule was infrequently violated, and very rarely with success. On practically every such occasion throughout history, the naval forces deliberately engaged the fortifications only when at least one of two conditions was met: (1) when the firepower of the attacking fleet was overwhelmingly superior to that of the shore defenses in terms of either the number or the caliber of its guns, or (2) when the attacking power had such overall naval superiority that it could afford to risk the loss of ships in order to attack or capture a coastal position of exceptional significance.

paralleled by few other nations. Here, as a recent American military historian has observed, the emphasis on this particular form of protection "was to grow virtually into an obsession" and lead, toward the end of the nineteenth century, to a program of harbor defense that became "almost a substitute for any other form of military policy."[3]

This concern with the fortification of seaports, which persisted as late as World War II, stemmed to some extent from the genuine defensive requirements imposed by this country's geography. Throughout its history, the powers that represented the most serious and most likely threats to its security lay across the seas rather than within this hemisphere. In addition, the United States, because of its extended coastlines and numerous coastal cities, simply had more points requiring such defense than did most other nations. These facts, however, cannot alone account for the American preoccupation with seacoast fortification, which must to a large degree be attributed to several long-enduring and interrelated attitudes and traditions, some dating back to our early colonial history. Most of these, basically unaltered with time except in terms of their specific end-products, still survive to affect today the steps being taken for national defense, much as they did a hundred years ago.

One such tradition is that of the militia concept and the related attitude of opposition to military professionalism and a large regular army. This concept was linked with defense against seaborne attack from the earliest colonial days, when the lack of military forces and the absence of reliable interior communications made it necessary for each settlement to prepare a battery of at least two or three guns that could be manned by the local populace in the event of danger from the sea. Although the provision of such defenses by individual communities came to an end shortly after the United States became a nation, the practice continued of preparing in peacetime defensive works that could be left idle and unmanned, except for purposes of maintenance, until they were needed.

Closely akin to the militia tradition is the American tendency to favor armaments of an economical sort, not solely or even primarily economical in the dollar sense, but rather in terms of personnel requirements. This bias toward forms of defense that require relatively few men even in war, and practically none in peacetime, was undoubtedly a major factor underlying the predisposition toward seacoast fortification. Of such defenses, wrote Lieutenant Henry W. Halleck in 1843—

When once constructed they require but little expenditure for their support. In time of peace they withdraw no valuable citizens from the useful occupations of life. Of themselves they can never exert an influence dangerous to public liberty;

3. Weigley, pp. 65, 144.

4

but as the means of preserving peace, and as obstacles to an invader, their influence and power are immense.[4]

Halleck's phrase, ". . . as the means of preserving peace," reflects still another attitude common among Americans, that security can be purchased —and mass mobilization avoided, perhaps entirely—by enough of the right kinds of military hardware. As war has grown in technical complexity, so has this attitude, and the obvious parallels between the seacoast fortifications, which are the subject of this book, and many of the post-World War II "weapons systems," in terms of the security promised by both, need hardly be pointed out.[5]

Finally, such defenses were patently nonaggressive in appearance and therefore appealed to one of the most deep-seated of this nation's traditions regarding war. They did not too seriously affront even those who most opposed war and who, so far as they condoned any form of military activity, tended to object least to ostensibly defensive modes of preparedness; nor did they offend those who, though not necessarily opposed to war as such, were distinctly opposed to foreign entanglements and any kinds of aggressive military activities that might lead to war.

This potent combination of traditions out of which our seacoast fortifications emerged, almost inevitably, as a foremost military tangible of the first century and a half of this nation's existence, was probably nowhere better articulated than in Grover Cleveland's annual message of December 1896:

We should always keep in mind that of all forms of military preparation coast defense alone is essentially pacific in its nature. While it gives the sense of security due to a consciousness of strength, it is neither the purpose nor the effect of such permanent fortifications to involve us in foreign complications, but rather to guarantee us against them. They are not temptation to war, but security against it. Thus, they are thoroughly in accord with all the traditions of our national diplomacy.[6]

Permanent seacoast fortification in the United States and the extent to

4. H[enry] Wager Halleck, "Report on the Means of National Defence," printed in S. Exec. Doc. 85, 28th Cong., 2d Sess., p. 9 (Serial 451). While still a relatively junior officer of Engineers, Halleck began to establish himself as a first-class military scholar through extensive writings. He became Secretary of State under the Military Governor of California, but left the Army in 1854 and entered law practice in San Francisco, where he specialized with great success in land cases involving Spanish and Mexican grants. Returning to the Army in 1861, he succeeded George B. McClellan as General-in-Chief a year later, and was in turn succeeded in 1864 by General Grant.

5. The persistence of this viewpoint was reaffirmed, as these pages were about to go to press, by Lieutenant General James M. Gavin, who, speaking on the matter of narrowly equating national security with an ever-growing amount of fighting hardware, described this as "working on the theory of . . . a giant armadillo." "The Military-Industrial Complex," *Newsweek*, June 9, 1969, pp. 83–84.

6. James D. Richardson, ed., *A Compilation of the Messages and Papers of the Presidents* (10 vols. and supplements; Washington: Government Printing Office [hereafter cited as GPO], 1907), vol. 9, pp. 728–729.

which it was pursued were thus justified at every turn through a faithful adherence to the notion that such construction offered the hope of avoiding war altogether. That this widely held view involved a vast oversimplification of certain military realities is beside the point; it was a view held by a sizable portion of the American public and by a succession of militarily naive Congresses, hence it materially affected the measures taken for national defense. Whether the fortifications in fact succeeded in their purpose is, of course, moot; the successful influence actually exercised by any so-called weapon of deterrence, by the inherent nature of such weapons, is rarely if ever determinable.

Tactics and Techniques

Construction of permanent seacoast fortifications in the United States was essentially a phenomenon of peacetime, and indeed, it constituted one of the Army's major activities between wars. Although harbor defense works were erected during every war, these were either built in continuation of a prewar program of permanent construction, or else they were rough, makeshift affairs that had little technical effect on the products of future peacetime construction. Only in the aftermath of the Civil War did the actual experiences of conflict have an appreciable influence on the design of subsequent defenses, and even in this instance the changes of the postwar period were due as much to the imposition of fiscal restraints as to any technical lessons of the war itself.

On the whole, the development of seacoast fortifications was a gradual process, punctuated only occasionally by a dramatic advance in armament technology or by the introduction of some new element, such as the airplane, into warfare. The general nature of such fortifications at any given time depended on a complex interrelationship of factors. The weight, range, and power of the armament available were, of course, among the foremost determinants, as were the characteristics of the enemy naval guns likely to be brought against them. These factors, in turn, depended on such things as the general state of the weaponry art, the capacity of industry to produce cannon of given calibers, lengths, and metals, and the chemistry of explosives. Also involved were developments in construction techniques, and improvements in the strength, durability, and resistance of building materials.

The specific number and type of fortifications required at a given time for the protection of a particular harbor depended on other variables, such as its commercial or naval importance, the depth and width of the channel, and the direction and velocity of the current (these were especially critical in the era of sailing vessels). The elevation and configuration of land adjoining a harbor also influenced the kinds of defenses to be constructed and their precise positioning.

Tactics and military-naval techniques also had an important effect upon the design and placement of defensive works. During the latter years of the era of smoothbore guns, for example, when red-hot cannonballs (hot shot) were commonly fired to ricochet along the water toward wooden ships, harbor defense structures were as a rule sited very near sea level. With the appearance of rifled guns in the late nineteenth century, however, batteries began to be raised, in some instances to positions several hundred feet above the water.

Out of the interaction of these various determinants, the seacoast fortifications constructed in this country between 1794 and World War II emerged in a succession of separate generations, each distinguished by a particular combination of building materials, armament, and architectural style. Of the eight such generations, the first four shared certain general features that distinguished them from the last four, and these two groups are therefore treated in separate major sections in the pages that follow.

The four early generations of defenses were constructed for the most part of earth, earth and stone, or entirely of stone or brick, and all were armed, almost without exception, with smoothbore cast-iron muzzle-loading cannon. The fifth generation and those following were based on rifled steel breech-loading guns of greatly increased power, and consisted of battery structures built primarily of reinforced concrete, frequently of enormous thickness.

One characteristic shared by all the defensive works was a high degree of architectural straightforwardness and simplicity, which is in large part responsible for the fact that the still-visible relics, to the average viewer, are almost impossible to date and, often, even to discriminate as to era. Such construction, as a rule, was remarkably free of the kind of ornamentation in which the most revealing clues to the age of any structure so often seem to be concentrated. Working within sometimes adequate but never lavish budgets that precluded nonessential adornment, the Army's engineers succeeded in producing seacoast fortifications that, compared to many contemporary civilian efforts—especially those of the late nineteenth century— were and still are models of architectural chastity.

Although fortifications designed to oppose naval forces were in many ways structurally different from those designed to protect inland positions, their overall function was basically that of all defensive works—first, to insure the retention of the fortified position and its denial to the enemy, and, second, to force the enemy to move into particular areas or along certain lines preselected by the defender. In these terms, seacoast forts had the primary function of insuring the security of commercial and naval harbors. In denying harbors to an enemy's fleet as well as to the shipping by which his invading troops might be supplied, the forts fulfilled their second function through forcing upon any waterborne invader the very costly necessity of coming ashore at highly unfavorable positions, such as an isolated open beach distant from any harbor with its sheltered waters and charted channels and such facilities as wharves and cargo-handling equipment.

Discussing this concept in 1851, the Army's Chief Engineer, Joseph G. Totten, presented it with a peculiarly American flavor:

In preparing against maritime assaults, the security of the points to be covered is considered to be greatly augmented whenever the defences can be so arranged as to oblige an enemy to land at some distance; for the reason that opportunity is thereby allowed, in the only possible way, for the spirit and enterprise of the people to come into play. Instead of being designed to prevent a landing on any part of the coast, as many seem to suppose, . . . the system [of seacoast fortifications] often leaves this landing as an open alternative to the enemy; and aims so to cover the really important and dangerous points, as to necessitate a *distant* landing [by the enemy] and a march towards the object, through the people.[7]

In other words, fortifications of the seacoast type were to a large measure intended to make the cost of any invasion so unattractive logistically as, hopefully, to discourage the undertaking altogether; or, failing that, to render the invasion as difficult and onerous as possible. For in the event of the enemy's successful debarkation at a point distant from his goal, "the resistance to his march may be safely left to the courage and patriotism that will find ample time to array themselves in opposition."[8]

Only once in modern times has an attempt been made to go beyond this principle of reliable defense of important harbors, and to insulate totally an extensive coastline by the installation of permanent defensive works. In this instance—Hitler's Atlantic Wall—even the staggering sums, materials, and forces invested were spread too thin in a failure that might well have been foreseen by any of several European military theorists of the eighteenth and nineteenth centuries.

It was one of these, Henri Lallemand—a former artillery general of Napoleon living in exile in the United States—who perhaps best summarized the realistic limits of coastal defense, as distinct from harbor defense, in a work prepared for use by the military forces of the new American republic:

It is not necessary to make of the coast a fortified line . . . No other plan, it is true, will prevent descents upon an extended coast, but it [is] impossible to pro-

7. J. G. Totten, *Report of the Chief Engineer on the Subject of National Defences* (Washington: A. Boyd Hamilton, 1851), pp. 5–6.
8. Ibid.

tect every point . . . All that can be done is to guard the most important positions . . .[9]

With the passage of time the most important positions—the well developed seaports and major river mouths—became progressively fewer as increased commerce demanded more spacious harbors and as new ships of larger dimensions reduced the number of entrance channels that could be traversed. Thus, in the early years of the nineteenth century fortifications could be found at about 35 separate coastal localities along the Atlantic from the Canadian border to Georgia (see Figure 1). But by 1850 the number of defended positions on this same section of the coast had been cut to about 20, in 1900 it was down to 16, and by 1940 there were but 10 permanently fortified positions between Maine and Savannah.[10]

The list of harbors requiring protection was likewise reduced as successive developments in the technology of armament led to increased effective ranges that enabled shore-mounted artillery to cover more extensive areas of water and span broader channels, often making it possible to dispense entirely with certain fortifications. At Chesapeake Bay, for instance, the emplacement after World War I of a battery of new weapons whose long-range fire could span the bay entrance from a position on Cape Henry permitted the elimination of two separate groups of older fortifications established more than a century earlier to guard different waterways within the bay. The former defenses of Baltimore and the Potomac—a total of six forts—were rendered superfluous by the single new installation which controlled the entrance to the entire body of Chesapeake Bay against hostile intrusion, whereas the previous defenses had guarded but small segments of the overall expanse of water.

More commonly, the introduction of armament with appreciably greater range simply reduced the number of forts and weapons needed for the protection of a given locality. By 1900, for example, only one heavy gun was needed for roughly every five emplaced in 1865. Between 1900 and 1945, the reduction in weapon requirements was even more marked, nearly tenfold, as illustrated by the situation at Narragansett Bay, where a twin-gun 16-inch battery was installed early in World War II at each side of the entrance, on Points Judith and Sakonnet. These four weapons supplanted a half-dozen separate forts, all well within the bay, whose armament in 1900 had comprised a total of more than three dozen heavy pieces. Aside

9. H. Lallemand, *A Treatise on Artillery* (New York: C. S. Van Winkle, 1820), vol. 2, pp. 103–104.

10. *American State Papers, Military Affairs* (7 vols.; Washington: Gales and Seaton, 1832–61), vol. 1, pp. 308–311 [hereafter cited as *ASP, MA*]; Totten, *National Defences,* pp. 51–53; Annual Report of the Chief of Engineers, U.S. Army, 1900, H. Doc. 2, 56th Cong., 2d Sess., p. 6 (Serial 4089) [hereafter cited in the form, *ARCE,* 1900, H. Doc. 2, 56/2 (Serial 4089)]; Stetson Conn, Rose C. Engelman, and Byron Fairchild, *Guarding the United States and Its Outposts* (volume in United States Army in World War II: The Western Hemisphere; Washington: Department of the Army, 1964), p. 47 (fn.).

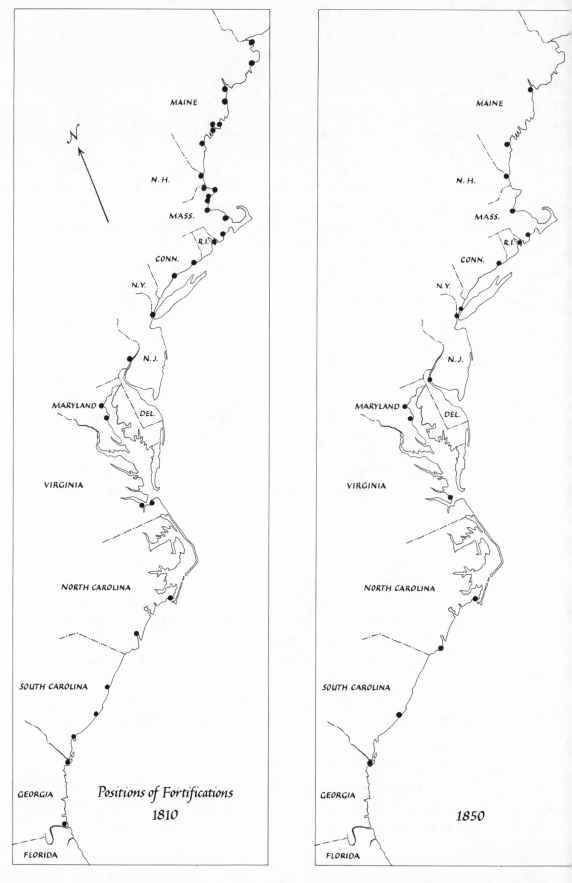

FIGURE 1. Maps showing progressive reduction in the number of fortified localities, 1810–1940.

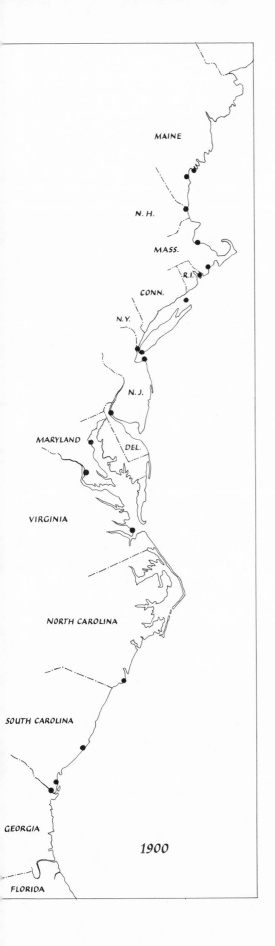

MAINE

N. H.

MASS.

R.I.

CONN.

N.Y.

N. J.

MARYLAND

DEL.

VIRGINIA

NORTH CAROLINA

SOUTH CAROLINA

GEORGIA

FLORIDA

1900

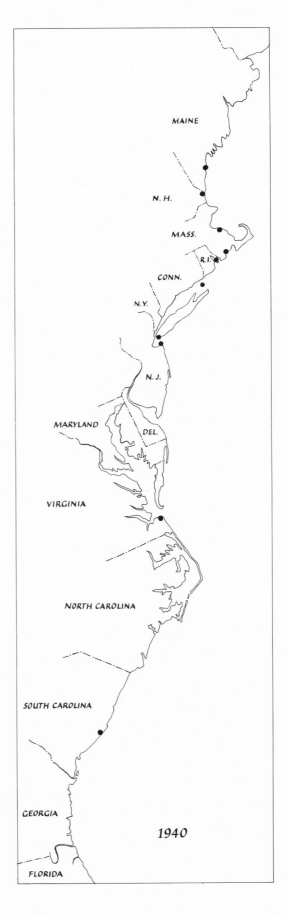

MAINE

N. H.

MASS.

R.I.

CONN.

N.Y.

N. J.

MARYLAND

DEL.

VIRGINIA

NORTH CAROLINA

SOUTH CAROLINA

GEORGIA

FLORIDA

1940

from their extended range, improved accuracy, and greatly increased armor-penetration capacity, the two new batteries met the defensive requirement formerly requiring nine batteries, and their installation thus effected a substantial economy in both supply and personnel. Even more striking was the gain at Puget Sound, where a single pair of World War II guns sited well out toward the ocean closed a large and complexly shaped water area that in 1900 had been guarded by over forty heavy weapons distributed among three forts.

As these examples suggest, the evolution of coastal weapons and the consequent increases in their range led to the construction of new lines of fortifications, each occupying sites progressively nearer to the ocean to permit hostile vessels to be brought under fire as far from land as possible. The earlier works, left behind in the process, were either relegated to limited service, literally as second lines of defense, or—as suggested in the instances described above—abandoned altogether.

This horizontal stratification of defensive works is fairly evident at most large harbors such as Boston, New York, and San Francisco, where the various lines of fortifications occupy a span of perhaps a dozen miles or less. But an even clearer example of the seaward shifting of artillery positions may be seen in Figure 2, which indicates the various points along the Delaware River at which defenses were located over a two-century period; for the geographical configuration of this waterway is such that each new stage of armament technology meant the relocation of fortification sites in increments not of 5 or 10, but of 40 or 50 miles.

Although several Dutch and Swedish forts were erected for local protection in this region during the 1600s, steps for the specific defense of Philadelphia against attack by water appear to date only from about 1750, when guns were first mounted on Society Hill, in the city's immediate vicinity. A quarter of a century later a position on Mud Island, a few miles below Philadelphia, was fortified on the eve of the American Revolution, and succeeding works on this site remained the principal protection against water-borne attacks until around 1820, when a permanent fort of the third generation was begun about forty miles down river on Pea Patch Island. This new line, eventually to consist of three forts, stood for almost exactly a century until, shortly after World War I, the protected perimeter was advanced an additional fifty miles or so seaward with the emplacement of four long-range guns on the Delaware shore east of Milford. Finally, during World War II, the entire water area of the river and its bay was defensively enclosed with the installation of a new pair of extremely powerful batteries on Cape Henlopen, some one hundred miles downstream from Philadelphia.[11]

11. Robert Arthur, "Coast Forts of Colonial New Jersey, Pennsylvania, and Delaware," *The Coast Artillery Journal* [hereafter cited as *CAJ*], vol. 69, no. 1 (July 1928), p. 56;

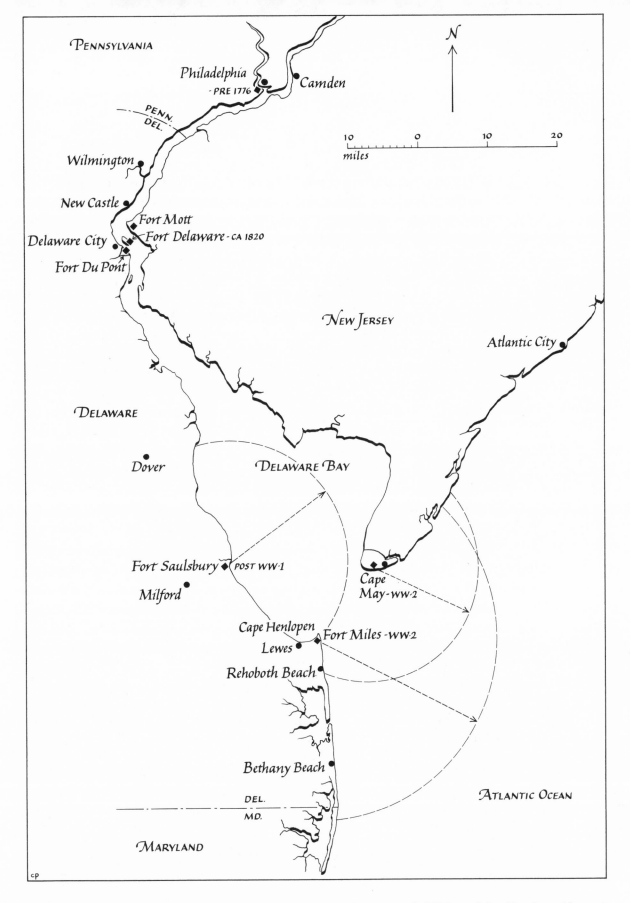

FIGURE 2. Map of the Delaware River region, showing the seaward shifting of fortifications (shown by diamonds) due mainly to advances in armament technology. Between 1800 and 1945, the effective range of coastal artillery increased by, roughly, a factor of 25, which meant not only that far wider channels could be defended, but also that the water area that could be covered from shore (as shown by arcs) increased more than six hundred times.

Colonial Beginnings

The widespread fortification of seaports, which began long before the American Revolution, stemmed in part from the geographical pattern of early colonization, which was determined largely by the nature of the Atlantic coastline. Because there were many sheltered bays, inlets, and river mouths, the settlements established by the various European nations in their efforts to gain footholds in the New World were numerous and widely dispersed along the coast rather than concentrated around a few large harbors. Moreover, the relative proximity of the Appalachian barrier tended to delay any mass movement toward the interior, with the result that the locus of colonization remained for some time at or near the coast. As a consequence, the sea was the primary avenue not only of supportive communication, but of potential attack as well, and the individual settlements had to provide for their own defense. Unlike the maritime nations of Europe, which as a rule erected seacoast forts only at their largest and most important commercial or naval harbors and which could rely on their standing military forces and established interior communications for the defense of lesser harbors, Colonial America had neither armies nor communications, and a large number of relatively insignificant coastal positions were therefore fortified.

Of these many works, the earliest was probably Charlesfort, built in 1562 by the Huguenot Jean Ribault on Parris Island, in what is now South Carolina.[12] Abandoned soon afterward upon the failure of the colony, this first example was followed over the next two hundred years by dozens of similar efforts undertaken in connection with various colonial and mercantile ventures. The builders included men of many nationalities—British, French, Spanish, Dutch, and Swedish—who often attempted in their designs to reproduce examples familiar to them from the Old World so far as the materials available to them permitted. Certainly no systematic pattern of defensive construction was adhered to.

Although it was an era during which the great military engineers of Europe were transforming the art of fortification into a science, their concern was mainly with large defensive works for the protection of important

---

ASP, MA, vol. 3, p. 259; W. Emerson Wilson, *Fort Delaware* (Newark: University of Delaware Press, 1957), p. 6; Reports of Completed Works, Coast Defenses of the Delaware (Batteries Hall and Haslet), and Harbor Defenses of the Delaware (Battery Construction Numbers 118 and 519), Record Group 77 (Records of the Office of the Chief of Engineers), National Archives. [National Archives material is hereafter cited in the form RG—, NA.]

12. Robert Arthur, "Colonial Coast Forts on the South Atlantic," *CAJ,* vol. 70, no. 1 (January 1929), p. 42.

inland positions, and their elaborate formalism offered little of practical value for the construction of tiny forts across the Atlantic to guard a sparse population against raids from the sea. Nevertheless, certain basic features were carried to America, though in a most rudimentary fashion. Thus, while seventeenth- and eighteenth-century works along the coast of the New World were often bastioned (i.e., built with prominences at their corners from within which small cannon could cover the outer faces of the main fort walls), their plans were as a rule products of gross trial and error that rarely exhibited any of the geometric intricacy so typical of contemporary European forts.

On the whole, the defenses constructed during this long colonial period were primitive affairs, simple and hastily built. Almost all were of earth, with or without supporting timber, though in certain of them a degree of durability was achieved by erecting parallel stone or brick walls twelve or fifteen feet apart and packing the intermediate space with earth or sand. Such a work was Fort George, of about a dozen guns, which for a brief period around 1735 was maintained on the Virginia site later occupied by Fort Monroe.[13] These early earthwork defenses were often used for but a short time and then abandoned to deteriorate, although a particularly favorable point on a harbor or river might, over many years, be alternately occupied and evacuated, thus serving as the site for a succession of works.

In a few such crucial locations defenses of substantial size were constructed out of more durable materials. Examples of these were the Spanish fort, begun in the 1670s at St. Augustine, and the large British work in Boston Harbor, completed just after 1700 and called Castle William in honor of William III. Both were basically rectangular structures with pronounced bastions at the angles, which gave them the appearance in plan that was to remain characteristic of major coastal forts until the early nineteenth century. The Spanish work (Figure 3), still in existence, was designed for about fifty guns and was constructed of coquina, a soft local stone of marine origin and suprising durability and resistance to cannon fire; Castle William, leveled after the American Revolution to make way for a new fort, was mainly of brick cemented with a mortar made from burnt oyster shells. Its armament of well over a hundred guns made it the most powerful fort in the British colonies.[14]

San Marcos and Castle William were clear exceptions to the general trend of defensive construction in the colonies, where small, inexpensive,

13. See, for example, Robert Arthur, *History of Fort Monroe* (Fort Monroe, Va.: The Coast Artillery School, 1930), p. 32.

14. Albert C. Manucy, *The Building of Castillo de San Marcos* (National Park Service Interpretive Series, History No. 1, Washington: GPO, n.d.), pp. 9–11, 30; Robert Arthur, "Coast Forts of Colonial Massachusetts," *CAJ*, vol. 58, no. 2 (February 1923), p. 115, David P. Kirchner, "American Harbor Defense Forts," *United States Naval Institute Proceedings,* vol. 84, no. 8 (August 1958), pp. 95ff.

FIGURE 3. The Castillo de San Marcos, at St. Augustine, Florida, is the oldest existing permanent seacoast fort in the continental United States. It was begun in 1672 on a site that had been occupied for about a hundred years by a succession of earth and wooden defensive works. Secured from Spain in 1821, when East Florida became part of the United States, it was renamed Fort Marion in honor of Francis Marion, the "Swamp Fox" of the American Revolution, and it remained in service throughout the nineteenth century, both as a defensive work and as a military prison. The fort became a national monument in 1924, and the original name, Castillo de San Marcos, was restored by Congress in 1942. The work is basically square in plan, with a large bastion protruding from each corner. As may be seen from the photo, the design of the bastions made it possible for every foot of the exterior wall to be swept by gunfire from within the structure. (Photo by Jack E. Boucher for HABS, National Park Service, 1965)

16

and highly perishable earthworks continued to be erected by individual communities for manning by local citizens in the event of peril from the sea. Weapons varied a great deal in size, but were generally of light caliber—24-pounder, 18-pounder, or smaller—except at a few of the permanent works, where the armament occasionally included cannon as large as 42-pounders.[15] The guns were often the kind used on board ships, many of them on four-wheel naval truck carriages, though some of the lighter pieces were undoubtedly mounted on two-wheel carriages of the sort employed by field artillery of the period.[16]

The Revolutionary War saw no appreciable advance in the nature of American coastal forts. During its seven years they naturally became more numerous, for works that had long been deteriorating were restored and many completely new ones erected, but their construction followed no uniform plan beyond the use of earth and timber or stone or whatever other suitable materials might be at hand, and the employment of any serviceable cannon, regardless of age, origin, pattern, or caliber. As a result, the defenses ranged in form from the most primitive of small linear batteries to infrequent efforts toward some measure of elegance. Representative of the latter extreme was Fort Whetstone (Figure 4), an unbastioned five-pointed earthwork near Baltimore (on the site subsequently occupied by Fort McHenry), one of the genuine examples among American harbor defense works of the so-called "star" forts.

At the close of the Revolution, a large number of works remained in existence; but over the next decade most of these simply went to pieces, for the individual states showed little interest in maintaining them. Thus, when the first national effort to fortify the harbors was undertaken in the 1790s, only three positions—Castle Island (Boston), Goat Island (Newport), and Mud Island (Philadelphia)—were found to have remnants worth repairing. In general, construction had to begin all over.[17]

15. When guns fired only solid, spherical shot (up to about the Civil War in the American service), their caliber was expressed in terms of the weight of the shot, hence 42-, 32-, 24-, and 18-pounder, equivalent, respectively, to bore diameters of 7, 6.4, 5.82, and 5.3 inches. The hollow, explosive-filled shells fired by mortars, howitzers, and columbiads, however, varied in weight even when of the same diameter because of differences in the thickness of the shell walls, and the caliber of such weapons—and subsequently that of guns as well—was expressed directly in inches. In the case of certain guns, and in some countries, the "pounder" designation remained in use well into the present century. The general trend at present is toward metric designations of diameter to express caliber.

16. Arthur, "Massachusetts," p. 115; Robert Arthur, "Coast Forts in Colonial New Hampshire," *CAJ*, vol. 58, no. 6 (June 1923), p. 551.

17. *ASP, MA,* vol. 1, pp. 62–63.

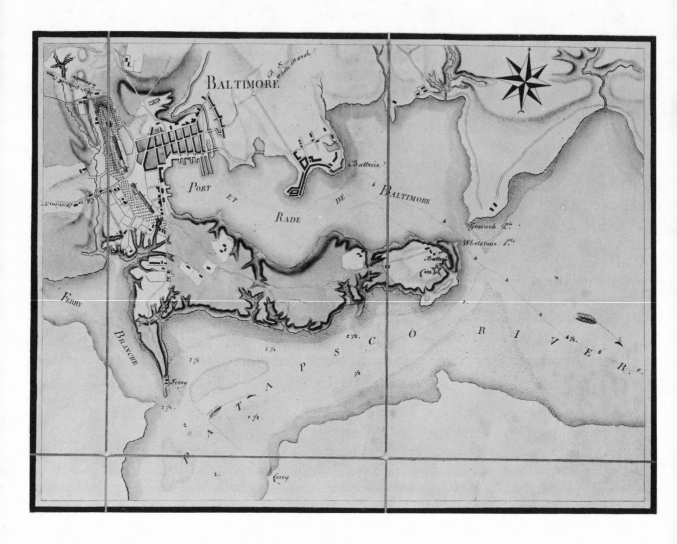

FIGURE 4. Fort Whetstone, Baltimore, was a five-pointed earthwork constructed probably during the summer of 1776. The oldest known drawing dates from about five years later and shows both the star fort and the separate shoreline battery erected a few months before the fort. In the 1790s the battery was repaired and the remnants of the fort were covered over by the construction of the present Fort McHenry. ("Ville, port et rade de Baltimore dans le Maryland" [assumed drawn 1781], in Rochambeau Collection, Library of Congress)

EARLY SYSTEMS:
Earthworks, Stone Forts, and Muzzle-Loaders

The European conflict following the French Revolution threatened more than once during the early 1790s to embroil the new United States and led President Washington repeatedly to urge upon Congress the need to provide defenses for its seaports. Finally, on February 28, 1794, a special committee of the House of Representatives submitted a statement of estimates and recommendations as to the kinds of works that should be erected and their locations.[18] On the basis of this report, the first federal authorization was passed within three weeks, on March 20.[19]

The Secretary of War at once issued instructions concerning the general character of the proposed fortifications, but left the specific plans and their execution to be worked out by the engineer at each locality. Because of the urgency and because funds were limited, construction was in all cases to be simple and inexpensive.[20] The results came to be known as the defenses of the First American System of fortifications—open works with earth parapets over which, depending on the size and importance of the harbor, from eight or ten to several dozen guns could fire. By contemporary European standards these defenses were weak and primitive. Some of them, where the soil lacked cohesiveness, had facing revetments of timber or, in rare instances, stone; but most were of unsupported earth, sodded or planted with knotgrass or some other binding growth. In addition to their major seaward battery, some of the forts included an enclosed earthen redoubt or a blockhouse with a light cannon or two to guard their landward sides.[21]

The harbor defense armament of this era consisted of a diverse collection of iron and brass cannon, most of which were Revolutionary War remnants. Some had been made in this country and others had been obtained from the French, but many of the pieces had been captured from the British. In age they ranged from some of fairly recent pattern and manufacture to others that were quite old, dating possibly from the early 1700s or even before.

With the exception of a few larger pieces, including perhaps a half-dozen 42-pounders, the heaviest weapons were 24-pounders, and many were of various smaller sizes. These, drawn in about equal numbers from federal

18. Ibid., pp. 61–64.

19. The Act of March 20, 1794, listed the positions to be fortified and the armament to be provided for this purpose (*U.S. Statutes at Large*, vol. 1, p. 345 [hereafter cited in the form 1 Stat. 345]). One further location, Annapolis, was added under 1 Stat. 367 (May 9, 1794). The initial appropriations were for $76,000 (construction) and $96,000 (armament), 1 Stat. 346 (March 21, 1794). The locations provided for are given in Appendix A.

20. Totten, *National Defences,* p. 50; *ASP, MA,* vol. 1, pp. 71–107.

21. *ASP, MA,* vol. 1, pp. 72ff., 78ff., 87ff., 93, 95.

arsenals and from stocks in the hands of the states, constituted a large part of the armament for First System defenses. Soon, however, they were augmented by new iron 32- and 24-pounders, manufacture of which had been authorized by the same legislation as the fortifications themselves.[22]

Uncertainty exists regarding the specific nature of gun carriages during this period; these, being of wood, tended to last only a few years, after which they were most likely replaced by later models. The fixed seacoast carriage which could traverse horizontally to allow its gun to follow moving targets was adopted from the French artillery system, but many pieces remained mounted on simple non-traversing carriages. "Traveling" carriages, heavier and less-mobile versions of the ordinary field-artillery mount, were also used, but four-wheel naval truck carriages almost certainly became less common at this time.

Inasmuch as the individual states furnished a substantial portion of the armament for the program, the effort was not exclusively a federal one. More important was the matter of government occupancy for defense purposes, which required either use permission or land cession by the several states, some of which retained ownership of the fortification sites until well into the nineteenth century. Moreover, the French engineers engaged to design and construct the defenses were at every stage required to secure approval of their plans by the state governors, whose own appointees generally had a considerable voice in questions of construction. Thus, though conceived, legislated, and basically outlined at the national level, the First System exhibited little in the way of overall design uniformity.[23]

Appropriations were modest and irregular, and the works for the most part were neither impressive nor durable. Within a short time exposure to the weather and lack of maintenance combined to reduce them to ruins. This rapid decay in the face of growing friction with France led Congress in 1798 to appropriate $250,000, a sum more than double any amount yet provided, to restore and complete certain of the existing works and to commence a small number of new ones. Further funds were provided during the four or five years that followed, and masonry materials began to appear in fair amounts as veneer and revetment, especially in some of the new forts commenced at this time.[24]

Of these new works, only a few survive to illustrate the final products of

22. The report of February 28, 1794 (cf. fn. 18) recommended the manufacture of one hundred each 24- and 36-pounders with carriages and 150 additional carriages for guns from the states. Of the 36-pounders, few if any were actually made. The Act of March 20, 1794 authorized only 24- and 32-pounders plus the additional carriages (cf. fn. 19).

23. See, for example, *ASP, MA,* vol. 3, pp. 582ff.; Arthur, *Fort Monroe,* p. 43; *ASP, MA,* vol. 1, pp. 72, 77, 87; and Edgar B. Wesley, "The Beginnings of Coast Fortifications," *CAJ,* vol. 67 (October 1927), pp. 283–284.

24. 1 Stat. 554 (May 3, 1798); *ASP, MA,* vol. 1, pp. 192–196.

FIGURE 5. Fort Mifflin, constructed between 1798 and 1803 for the defense of Philadelphia, was located on Mud Island at the confluence of the Schuylkill and Delaware Rivers, on a site first fortified about 1775. Built on an unusual plan that had features of both star and bastion designs, the work was named for Major General Thomas Mifflin, Continental Army. (For a comment on the naming of forts, see footnote 25 on page 25.) Like many of the early nineteenth century coastal forts, it was intermittently garrisoned, and was sometimes left to caretaker detachments for periods of 10 or 15 years. Vacated by regular troops in the mid-1850s, the fort was again occupied by Volunteer forces during the Civil War but shortly afterward was once more abandoned. Throughout most of the present century it was used by the Navy Department as an ammunition depot. (Photo, courtesy U.S. Naval Institute, 1961)

FIGURE 6. Fort McHenry, probably the best known of American coastal forts, was constructed about 1800 to guard the harbor of Baltimore. Located on Whetstone Point, the fort was greatly strengthened by the addition of exterior batteries during the War of 1812 and the Civil War. For a period of 25 hours on September 13 and 14, 1814, 16 British warships bombarded the fort with artillery and rockets, but it withstood the attack, inspiring Francis Scott Key's poem, *The Star-Spangled Banner*. Most of the exterior batteries presently flanking the fort were erected much later, around the time of the Civil War. Named for James McHenry, Secretary of War from 1796 to 1800, this work was designated as a National Monument and Historic Shrine by Congress in 1939. (Smithsonian Institution photo, 1963)

the First System, the first defenses of any permanence to be erected by the United States. Two good examples may be seen in Fort Mifflin near Philadelphia and Fort McHenry in Baltimore, both of which remain essentially unaltered from their original form (Figures 5 and 6).[25]

Shortly after 1800, the fortifications began once more to lapse into disrepair. No building appropriations of any consequence were made for several years, and the funds for upkeep were insignificant. Most of what was available went to completing and maintaining the works at the three or four locations of primary importance. But as the threat of a second war with Great Britain grew, especially after the *Chesapeake* incident of June 1807, attention turned again toward harbor defense. A new fortification project was drafted in November 1807, and the next five years brought the remarkable total of more than three million dollars in appropriations for its implementation.[26] This program of construction got under way rapidly and was well advanced by the outbreak of war in 1812. Its products, which came to be known as the defenses of the Second System, were on the whole more elaborate than those of the First. They continued, however, to reflect limited coordination in planning, with the result that the armament and the architectural style of the works showed considerable variation. In one important respect the second program differed significantly from that begun in 1794 and represented an historical landmark for both the Army and the country as a whole: it was the first construction effort of any magnitude to be planned and carried out by engineers of American birth and training.[27]

Three general kinds of defensive works were included within the new system: open batteries, masonry-faced earth forts, and all-masonry forts. The last of these, none of which had been included in the First System, were to constitute a major turning point in American military architecture.

25. In some instances the origins of many early fort names cannot be positively identified because of an absence of documentation, in others because the formal naming order merely specified the designation officially to be used but did not identify the individual being honored. Not until the late nineteenth century did the naming authority begin as a rule to identify explicitly the person for whom a fort was being named.

26. *ASP, MA,* vol. 1, pp. 219–222. The proposals listed not only defenses for more than fifty localities (many of which were not, in fact, to be fortified), but also a total of 257 gunboats in addition to fifty authorized the previous year. The initial appropriation for this program (2 Stat. 453 [January 8, 1808]) was for one million dollars, a sum four times as large as any previously given, and one not to be exceeded by a single appropriation until 1836. Further prewar funds were authorized by 2 Stat. 516 (February 10, 1809), 547 (June 14, 1809), 661 (March 3, 1811), and 692 (March 10, 1812).

27. Unlike the contract engineers, mainly French, who had built the works of the First System, these men were regular officers of the Army, most of them freshly out of the new academy at West Point. It had been established in 1802 primarily for the training of engineers in this country so that "we may avoid the unpleasant necessity of employing Foreigners as Engineers" (Letter, Secretary of War Henry Dearborn to Decius Wadsworth, June 21, 1803, 58510/41, RG 77, NA).

The open batteries, built in a variety of shapes (linear, polygonal, curved), were low, generally small works erected either in positions of secondary importance or near a fort as supporting adjuncts. Developmentally they were relatively insignificant, for similar batteries were included in most harbor defense programs. Nor were they especially durable, and those remaining are difficult to identify with certainty as belonging to this period.

The second group of works, the masonry-faced forts, comprised the greater part of the major defenses built during these years. In terms of materials and construction methods they did not differ greatly from the forts completed in the latter part of the First System era, only a half-dozen years earlier. Their design, however, was distinguished by the frequency with which the plans of post-1807 forts included circular or elliptical segments.[28] Among the defenses erected on Staten Island during the War of 1812, for example, were Fort Richmond, a semicircular structure, and Fort Tompkins, a regular pentagon with circular bastions (Figure 7). Though built by the State of New York (and later taken over by the United States), these works were basically of the Second System style. Despite the large number of masonry-faced works constructed during this period, few survive in anything like their original form, for most of them, like the remnants of the First System, disappeared during the third era, when they were either modified extensively or demolished entirely and replaced by newer structures. This appears to have been especially true of the pre-1812 forts constructed with curved faces, of which one remaining example may be seen at Fort Norfolk in Virginia, a complexly shaped structure completed about 1809 (Figure 8) which included a main battery of semielliptical form.[29]

More nearly resembling the defenses of the previous generation were a small number of bastioned and star forts of earth and masonry. Representative of the former type and among the largest in size is Fort Columbus (or Fort Jay) on Governors Island in New York Harbor (Figure 9), which was built in the form of a square with pronounced bastions. Actually begun in the 1790s and more or less under continuous construction for several years thereafter, it was given its principal masonry support as part of the 1807 project.

A few non-bastioned star forts also appeared during this era, but these too tended to fall to make way for works of the next generation. The best remnant of this variety is Fort Wood on Bedloe's Island, a unique eleven-pointed specimen which now serves as the base of the Statue of Liberty (Figure 10). Built prior to 1812, this work was structurally improved in the early 1840s when its exterior scarp was reinforced with granite and raised a few feet. But unlike most reconstructed forts of the same period,

28. *ASP, MA,* vol. 1, pp. 308–311.
29. Totten, *National Defences,* pp. 51–52; *ASP, MA,* vol. 1, p. 310.

FIGURE 7. Forts Tompkins and Richmond overlook the Narrows leading into New York Harbor. In this engraving of the 1850s, the original Fort Tompkins, with its circular bastions of the 1812 era, stands atop the hill at the left, as does a semaphore used to signal the sighting of ships and their approach. Old Fort Richmond, a semicircular work of the same period, was demolished to make room for the new fort, begun in 1847 and shown under construction near the channel. Within a few years Fort Tompkins also was to be replaced by a newer work (see Figures 29 and 47). At the extreme right of the picture is Fort Lafayette, begun in 1812 on Hendrick's Reef just off the Long Island shore of the Narrows. *(Gleason's Pictorial,* Nov. 27, 1852)

FIGURE 8. Fort Norfolk, Virginia. Of the several harbor defense forts constructed with semicircular or semielliptical faces during the pre-1812 period, this is the only work that survives in good condition and basically in its original form. Completed about 1809 to replace an earlier fort of the same name built under the 1794 program, Fort Norfolk was turned over to the Navy Department in 1824. It was occupied by Confederate troops in 1861 but was retaken by Federal forces a year later and garrisoned until transferred again to the Navy in 1864. The site is presently maintained by the Corps of Engineers. (Photo, U.S. Army Corps of Engineers, Norfolk District, about 1965)

FIGURE 9. Fort Columbus in New York Harbor was constructed on Governors Island over a work of the First System that had been commenced here in 1794 and named in honor of John Jay, first Chief Justice of the United States. The earlier work had been expanded and improved more or less continuously until about 1806, but it was finally demolished to a large degree to make way for the 100-gun bastioned fort shown here. As a harbor defense work, Fort Columbus remained occupied only until the 1850s, but it continued to serve for over a hundred years more as a headquarters post for various commands, and in 1904 the fort, along with the rest of the reservation, was officially renamed Fort Jay. In 1966 the headquarters of the First U.S. Army was moved from the New York area and Governors Island was declared surplus. (Photo, U.S. Army Air Corps, 1932)

Figure 10. The term "star fort" has often been used loosely to refer to practically any work, such as Fort McHenry (see Figure 6), built roughly in the form of a star. True star forts, which had no bastions, were relatively rare in the United States, particularly after 1800, when this type of plan began to be abandoned because of the difficulty of protecting the major exterior faces of forts built in this style. The star concept remained in limited use for another two decades or so, however, mostly in the design of island forts, where defense against attack by land was not a major consideration. Shown here is an outstanding example, Fort Wood, on Bedloe's (now renamed Liberty) Island in New York Harbor, named for Brevet Lieutenant Colonel Eleazer D. Wood, U.S. Army, who was killed in action at Fort Erie, Upper Canada, in 1814. Repaired and slightly modified in the 1840s, it remained in harbor defense service until work began in the early 1880s on the Statue of Liberty. (Photo 61-JB-0763, National Park Service, 1961)

Fort Wood has retained its original basic form despite these and other changes.[30]

In terms of its contribution to the development of fortification technology in the United States, the most significant product of the Second System was the all-masonry fort. This type of construction, together with the adoption of the casemated gun emplacement, opened the entire era of high, vertical-walled harbor defenses in this country. The casemate emplacement, by far the most important element yet to appear in American military architecture, permitted the mounting of seacoast cannon within a fort, rather than atop its exterior walls.

The basic idea of firing through embrasures in the external wall of a fort was not new. Loopholes had long been provided for bowmen and hand gunners, and for perhaps three hundred years light cannon had been mounted within bastion casemates to protect the exterior faces of forts. Even the casemating of heavy guns had been tried in a few seacoast forts built around 1540 by Henry VIII of England, but firing such large weapons within closely confined spaces had created numerous technical difficulties. These soon prompted a return to the usual practice of mounting a fort's principal armament in the barbette manner to fire over the outer walls, and it was not until some two hundred years later, during the 1780s, that the casemate was successfully reintroduced into harbor defense construction by the French engineer Montalembert, whose new designs solved most of the earlier problems.[31]

Although the most apparent benefit gained in adopting this innovation was the increased protection it afforded both guns and gunners from enemy fire, its real military advantage lay in its making possible the arrangement of a fort's armament in multiple tiers, much as the guns of contemporary ships were stacked on two or three decks. As a result, the volume of fire attainable from a work of a given plan area could be increased manyfold, and a fair concentration of firepower over a channel could be attained with one or two comparatively small forts.

This new element of defensive design did not come into general use in the United States until after 1816. It was, however, several years earlier that construction had begun at New York and Charleston, South Carolina, on the original American works to be planned around the casemate concept.

The largest of these was built between 1807 and 1812 on the north point of Governors Island, New York Harbor, by Colonel Jonathan Wil-

30. Various plans, drawings in Drawer 38, RG 77, NA, Cartographic Branch.
31. W. G. Ross, *Textbook of Fortification and Military Engineering for Use at the Royal Military Academy* (Woolwich: Her Majesty's Stationery Office, 1886), part 2, p. 204; Henry L. Abbot, *Course of Lectures Upon the Defence of the Sea-Coast of the United States* (New York: Van Nostrand, 1888), p. 139.

liams, the United States Army's first Chief Engineer. Named in his honor (and not to be confused with the old British Castle William at Boston), Castle Williams was designed with four levels on a basically circular plan about 210 feet in diameter (Figure 11). Each of its two lower casemate tiers had 26 gun positions, while the third level was to serve as a bomb-proof barracks for three hundred men or, if necessary, as the site of 26 additional guns. It was originally intended to mount 48 lighter cannon on the "terrace" or barbette tier, but in the course of construction this space was given to 26 new weapons of the heaviest caliber.[32]

As completed, Castle Williams had approximately 80 guns (the number was subsequently increased to 102), which, together with its design, made it easily the most formidable seacoast defense work yet built in the United States. More important, as the most advanced product of this period it became the prototype of all major coastal forts to be constructed in the United States over the following half century.

The guns of the Second System forts and batteries did not differ basically from those of the preceding period in terms of design or operation, but because the production of new cannon at this time included many of greater size, the overall average of the armament was increased in terms of caliber. The marked confusion of the 1790s as to types and sizes was reduced, more-over, as the supply of new guns made it possible to discard many of the existing pieces, particularly those made of brass, those of odd calibers, and those that were very old. Although seacoast armament was not to be gen-uinely systematized until about 1840, the trend toward standardization of patterns and calibers was also furthered during this period by the appear-ance, beginning around 1800, of the first literature on heavy ordnance in nearly a quarter of a century to become available in this country.[33]

Among the newly manufactured guns, the heaviest were some fifty or sixty pieces about evenly distributed between two types. Roughly half were iron 42-pounders, possibly of French pattern but cast in the United States. Practically all of these went into the arming of Castle Williams, as did about two dozen new 50-pounders of American design known as "columbiads."[34]

32. *ASP, MA,* vol. 1, pp. 237, 246, 309.
33. Among the most widely used of the works which included the materiel (as opposed to the operation and tactics) of artillery were William Stevens's *A System for the Disci-pline of the Artillery of the United States of America, or, The Young Artillerist's Pocket Companion,* printed in New York in 1797; a translation from the French by Jonathan Williams of a work by M. de Scheel, published in Philadelphia in 1800 as *A Treatise of Artillery Containing a New System, or, The Alterations Made in the French Artillery Since 1765;* and Louis de Tousard's *American Artillerist's Companion,* published at Phila-delphia in two volumes of text in 1809 and an additional volume of plates in 1813.
34. *The Columbiad* was the title of a poem by Joel Barlow after which the new 50-pounder is generally supposed to have been named. There is evidence, however, to

The latter were developed around 1810 or 1811 by a young engineer, George Bomford, who two decades later was to become the head of the Army's Ordnance Department. Surprisingly little is known about the history or the characteristics of this weapon, particularly in view of the fact that it subsequently came to be regarded as the first major American contribution to the worldwide development of artillery materiel and perhaps was the actual basis for the celebrated shell gun introduced into warfare by (and named for) the French officer Henri-Joseph Paixhans during the 1820s. It is known that the columbiad was designed to use not only solid shot (as did all large-caliber guns of that period) but explosive shell as well, which at that time were not ordinarily fired by heavy guns, but only at high angles by mortars and howitzers using reduced propelling charges.[35]

Concerning the details of gun carriages during this period, as in that preceding, comparatively little information is available, but because of the increase in the number of permanent works and in the proportion of heavy cannon, there is no doubt that the traversing seacoast type was more widely used than before. No standard pattern existed, however, and the carriages built for one fort would not necessarily fit the emplacements of another.[36] Although detailed drawings appear in a few of the books mentioned above, it is not clear whether these were meant to represent carriages actually in use or merely to serve as guides to be followed in manufacture.

With the lighter guns, two-wheeled mobile carriages continued to be employed, and replicas of these exist in fair numbers (examples may be seen at Fort McHenry). But of heavy wooden coast carriages there are no known reconstructions of unquestionable accuracy. It is not unlikely, however, that many followed the general design (see Figure 13) presented in the work of Tousard, which was published in three volumes between 1809 and 1813.[37]

Most of the defenses constructed under the program begun in 1807 were essentially finished by the outbreak of hostilities in 1812. Others were

suggest a different origin and usage: that the name was also applied—at least for a time—to any cannon manufactured by Henry Foxall's Columbian Foundry at Georgetown, D. C. It was certainly used to designate other types of cannon (see, for example, *ASP, MA*, vol. 3, p. 913).

35. Explosive shells were, at this time, known as "bombs," hence Francis Scott Key's ". . . bombs bursting in air, . . ." There is some suggestion that a new type of shell, elongated in form, was secretly developed for but never used with the columbiads (see the *Army and Navy Journal*, November 26, 1864, p. 214).

36. Letter, Lt. Col. George Bomford to P. B. Porter, Secretary of War, February 27, 1829, in *A Collection of Annual Reports and Other Important Papers Relating to the Ordnance Department* (4 vols.; Washington: GPO, 1878–1890), vol. 1, pp. 187–188 [hereafter cited as *Ord. Rpts. & Papers*].

37. Louis de Tousard, *American Artillerist's Companion* (Philadelphia: Bradford and Inskeep, Newyork [sic], 1813), vol. 3.

FIGURE 11. The construction of Castle Williams on Governors Island introduced into American military engineering the casemate emplacement for heavy guns, making possible the arrangement of the principal defensive armament in multiple tiers. With walls of red sandstone 40 feet high and 7 to 9 feet thick, this structure, begun in 1807, became the prototype of the major seacoast forts built in this country prior to the Civil War. It was named for its designer, Jonathan Williams, first superintendent of West Point, and it served not only in harbor defense but, during the Civil War and again beginning in 1912, as a military prison. With the rest of Governors Island, Castle Williams was declared surplus by the Army in 1966. (Photo, U.S. Army, about 1960)

Facing page

FIGURE 12. Castle Clinton, New York City, was begun shortly after Castle Williams and was planned as a companion defensive structure, but it was never raised beyond the first tier of emplacements. Originally known as "West Battery," and renamed in 1815 to honor Governor DeWitt Clinton, it was the last of the series of forts that since the 1620s had been located at the foot of Manhattan Island. Its brief military service ended in 1823, when it was transferred to the City of New York. Subsequently an entertainment center, as Castle Garden for three decades it provided the stage for music, drama, and oratory: here in 1850 P. T. Barnum first presented Jenny Lind to an American audience. Five years later the structure became an immigration depot and remained in this service for about 35 years, until the opening of the Ellis Island facility. From 1896 it housed the New York City Aquarium, which was removed to Coney Island just prior to World War II. The Castle Clinton National Monument was established in 1950. (Photos 61-JB-742 and 748, National Park Service, 1961)

completed during the war years that followed, many were strengthened by the addition of further batteries, and several new temporary works were provided at various positions. Thus, by 1815 practically every seaport of any consequence in the United States had at least one or two fortifications as part of a moderately respectable, though necessarily mixed assemblage of roughly sixty separate First and Second System defenses of varying size, style, and strength. A tabulation of these defended positions appears in Appendix A.

The first two fortification programs had been initiated under similar circumstances of impending conflict and pursued throughout periods of continuing uncertainty, with an emphasis on urgency that tended in each case to overshadow other considerations. As a result the works of both Systems were built rapidly, even the largest and most substantial being completed within three or four years. Neither program as a whole lasted more than ten years, since both slowed virtually to a halt once the imminence of war had diminished appreciably. In short, these efforts, despite the permanent character of a few of their products, were basically emergency undertakings.

The following era of construction, in marked contrast, was to continue for almost exactly half a century and the building of some of its individual works was to proceed methodically for two decades or more; for it began in the wake of a war whose events, including the burning of the national capital, provided an impact that dramatically reinforced the American penchant for safeguarding the maritime frontier and elevated seacoast fortification from the status of an emergency measure to a position of foremost importance among this nation's major methods of defense.

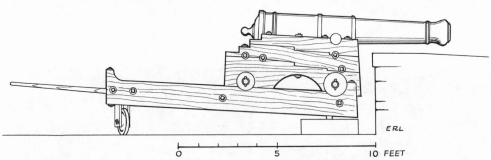

FIGURE 13. Seacoast gun and carriage of the 1812 period. On firing, the gun and upper carriage rolled to the rear and upward along the inclined rails of the chassis. In this rearward position, the weapon was loaded for the next round, then returned with handspikes or block and tackle to the forward position for firing. The chassis (the lowest portion of the gun carriage) was mounted within the emplacement on two wheels at the rear and a pintle at the front around which it could be swiveled laterally to follow moving targets. (Drawing, after Tousard, by author)

Unlike the first two periods of fortification, both of which, as noted, were undertaken while the possibility of a war threatened, the third was begun in 1817 under relatively tranquil circumstances. Immediacy was no longer an overriding consideration, and attention could be directed at last to the creation of a permanent and truly integrated system of harbor defenses.

Up to this time specific plans and designs had been prepared by individual engineers who had worked independently of each other under quite general instructions issued directly by the Secretary of War. No intermediate professional body had existed in the War Department during those years to coordinate planning, to determine project standards, or to supervise the actual construction.

As a consequence, the First System was not at all a true system with regard to the nature of its components, which were neither uniform nor durable. And the Second, though it included several substantial works, was marked by a dissimilarity among its elements, e.g., between the conventional and the new casemated types, that was far more basic and evident than any common characteristic serving to distinguish them, as a group, from the products of earlier or later periods. Nor was either of these Systems viewed as systematic (in the sense of constituting a cohesive and mutually supporting body of defenses) by the special board of officers convened expressly to create a third, "permanent," and genuine system of defenses under a long-term program of construction that was to continue until the Civil War.[38]

This group was placed in charge of the entire undertaking with responsibility for designating the positions requiring fortification, arranging these in order of their relative importance, determining general design characteristics, and reviewing the specific site selections and actual plans of the engineers in charge of the various works. For the first time, a professionally competent authority had been established to direct virtually all aspects of seacoast fortification design and construction. In one form or another, and under a variety of names, such a body was to remain in existence until the beginning of World War II.

Organized late in 1816, the Board was headed by a French military engineer, Simon Bernard, who had served as a brigadier general under Napoleon, and who had come with Lafayette's recommendation to the United States, where he was given a brevet commission in the same grade. The other members were one naval officer and two engineers of the Army, among them Brevet Lieutenant Colonel Joseph G. Totten, destined to

38. *ASP, MA,* vol. 2, p. 305.

become a world figure in the development of nineteenth-century seacoast fortification and one of the leading military engineers in American history.[39]

Although the concern of the Bernard Board was to be narrowed in time to fortification as such, it originally had the far more comprehensive task of dealing with seacoast defense in its broadest terms, as an activity involving the efforts of several interrelated elements—a navy, fortifications, avenues of communication in the interior, and a regular army and well-organized militia. Thus, the members were occupied from the outset with a thorough inspection not only of the coast, but of land and water routes in the interior as well. They traveled extensively, conferring with local engineers and examining dozens of positions in detail, and gradually developed projects for the protection of each of the various coastal regions. In a few critical locations defenses were begun even as the survey proceeded.[40]

The Board's first complete report was submitted in February 1821. Noting the primacy of the Navy in a total system of defense, it began by indicating the locations to be utilized for such facilities as major bases, repair yards, and anchorages. It then turned specifically to the fortifications required to guard both these facilities and the many commercial seaports, river mouths, and other important coastal localities. Its specific recommendations were comparatively modest; only 18 defensive works were listed in the first class, "of the most urgent necessity," but an additional 32 were projected for future construction under two further categories of lesser priority.[41]

At first the Board's attention was devoted primarily to getting work started in certain crucial positions and to getting the program as a whole under way. But as it turned gradually to long-range planning, the Board began to propose new items in ever increasing numbers. Ultimately, by about 1850, Bernard, his colleagues, and their successors were to draft a most ambitious scheme of harbor defense for the United States. Nearly two

39. Bernard was commissioned by President Madison on November 16, 1816, the same day that the Board was appointed by Acting Secretary of War George Graham. See Special Orders, No. 221–0, War Department, September 20, 1920; Ralston B. Lattimore, *Fort Pulaski National Monument, Georgia* (National Park Service Historical Handbook Series, Number 18, Washington: GPO, 1954), p. 5; Arthur, *Fort Monroe*, p. 38. Unlike the other members of the original Board, all of whom left it for one reason or another within a few years, Totten remained directly involved with the development, planning, and construction of seacoast fortifications for the remainder of his professional life, which coincided almost exactly with the era of the Third System. When he died in 1864, while in his twenty-sixth year as the Army's Chief Engineer, the era was just coming to a close. Because of his singular influence on this generation of defenses and the continuity that he, far more than any other individual, provided for its realization, the Third System was often referred to by later engineers as the Totten System.

40. *ASP, MA,* vol. 2, pp. 305, 312; Arthur, *Fort Monroe,* p. 39.

41. *ASP, MA,* vol. 2, pp. 308, 310–311.

hundred separate works were envisioned, guarding practically every harbor from Eastport, on the Maine-Canadian border, to the bay mouths of western Louisiana, three locations on the Gulf in Texas, and about twenty positions along the Pacific coast between San Diego and Puget Sound.[42] Actually this enormous program of fortification was never realized nor were most of the defenses even commenced. As was to be the case with practically every subsequent harbor defense effort, the gap between the number of works built and those projected grew steadily larger as the program proceeded. In practice, construction tended to center around the principal harbors, largely in the replacement or restoration of older works. Of the many new locations that were to have been fortified for the first time, only a few (mainly in Florida and along the Gulf coast) were actually provided with Third System defenses.

In the Bernard Board's initial report of 1821, the works of the First and Second Systems were barely mentioned; clearly they were to play no part in future harbor defense except, perhaps, to furnish some degree of protection until the new forts were completed. Within a few years, however, a small number of the old works began to be marked for incorporation into the new program, some to be modified in the process. The rest were to be "preserved, but not as part of the system," keeping their original form until, presumably, they were either demolished to make way for new works or simply abandoned. But as time passed, an increasing number of the pre-1816 defenses were repaired or modified, until about two dozen of the reconstructed old forts—among them a few which had been secured in the course of the Louisiana and Florida acquisitions—came to be included.[43]

New works of the Third System proper were built in a variety of forms. The least elaborate, as in the earlier periods, were the numerous detached batteries. Since these were relatively inexpensive and could be completed in a short time, they were often erected in locations of secondary importance, where the expense of a major fort was not justified. Others were built to provide interim defense while a fort was under construction nearby. Some of those that remained to serve as ancillary works may still be seen in the vicinity of major fort structures.

Batteries of this era were generally linear in plan, though a few were circular, semicircular, or crescent-shaped. Occasionally they were quite large, comprising as many as twenty or more guns in an uninterrupted row. Most were of the simple barbette variety in which the armament was mounted, without overhead cover, behind a brick- or stone-backed parapet of earth (Figure 14). Some, however, were considerably more elaborate, consisting

42. Totten, *National Defences,* pp. 51–55, 75–76, 88–89.
43. *ASP, MA,* vols. 2, pp. 310–312; 3, pp. 257–260; Totten, *National Defences,* pp. 92–95.

FIGURE 14. In this photo, taken about 1930, open barbette batteries flank Fort Independence on Castle Island, Boston, one of the oldest fortified sites in the United States. The 10-gun battery on the left was designed and constructed around 1840, though the four guns mounted in it are of Civil War vintage. The two pairs of empty emplacements to the right of the fort are products of the early 1870s. The original Fort Independence, built after the American Revolution on the site of the British Castle William, was named in August 1799 on the occasion of a visit by President Adams to Castle Island. In 1800 the present fort was begun, designed principally by Jean Fontin, a French engineer who shortly before had been involved in the planning and construction of Fort McHenry, Baltimore. Fort Independence was one of several First and Second System works modernized during the 1830s and 1840s to supplement the new forts of the Third System, and during this period it underwent considerable modification. (Photo 17178 AC, U.S. Army Air Corps, about 1930)

FIGURE 15. The 40-gun casemated water battery at Fort Monroe extended along the southeast side of the moat surrounding the fort and provided heavy armament at water level (see footnote 54, page 58). Prior to the Civil War it was armed with 42-pounder (7-inch) guns, but these were replaced during the 1860s with 10-inch weapons that fired projectiles of about 125 pounds. Some of the 10-inch guns, similar to but smaller than the piece shown in Figure 34, remained in the battery until around 1900. (Photo, in author's collection, of drawing, probably early 1870s)

FIGURE 16. Among the several Martello towers erected in this country prior to the Civil War, designs and modes of construction varied considerably. Unlike those along the south and east coasts of England, which were built in large numbers to a standard design shortly after 1800, towers in the United States followed no fixed pattern. The particular example shown here was located on Tybee Island, Georgia, as part of the defenses of the Savannah River. Others, some quite different in style, were built in several states, including Louisiana, Florida, South Carolina, and New Hampshire. (Photo 77-F-68-30, in the records of the Chief of Engineers, National Archives)

of a single tier of casemate emplacements (Figure 15) in which the guns were provided with bomb-proof cover in the form of a roof supported by masonry arches.[44]

A design of an entirely different sort was followed in a very few instances, mostly in the South, in the construction of tower batteries. Noteworthy as architectural curiosities, these small works were rectangular or circular in plan and mounted only a few pieces arranged to provide all-round fire. Commonly known as Martello towers (Figure 16), a name inspired by the remarkable performance in 1794 of a somewhat similar structure on the Bay of Martello in Corsica, many such batteries had been built prior to 1812 in both the Western Hemisphere and other parts of the world, but examples were extremely rare during this early period in the United States.[45]

It was among the principal forts of the Third System, however, that some of the most spectacular harbor defense structures to come out of any era of military architecture were to be found. Included by virtue of their role in the Civil War were certainly some of the most famous—Sumter, Pulaski, Monroe, Pickens, Morgan, and Jackson. From the technical standpoint, this large group of massive, vertical-walled forts represented the general embodiment and the fullest development of features which had previously appeared in only a few isolated instances, i.e., structural durability, a high concentration of armament, and enormous overall firepower.

The material permanence of seacoast defenses was always an elusive ideal. Because of their location such works were constantly subjected to the unusually potent erosive action of storms and waves, and their durability depended in effect on the availability of funds and of personnel for their maintenance. Since neither ever amounted to much in the United States except in times of war, and since works built even partially of earth were especially perishable, it was essential in the interests of long-term preparedness (and economy) that the fortifications be made as lasting as it was possible to make them, and that such works be commenced at the earliest opportunity.

For reasons already suggested, it was not until a period of reduced

44. Miscellaneous plans, RG 77, NA, Cartographic Branch.

45. The Martello episode is described in H. Wager Halleck, *Elements of Military Art and Science; or, Course of Instruction in Strategy, Fortification, Tactics of Battles, &c.* (New York: D. Appleton & Co., 1846), pp. 164–165. The English ships *Fortitude* (74 guns) and *Juno* (32 guns) were repelled and considerably damaged by fire from the tower, which had one barbette-mounted gun. The *Fortitude* lost seven men and was set on fire repeatedly. None of the tower's thirty or so men, only three of whom were needed to operate the single defensive weapon, were lost. For comments on towers in the Western Hemisphere, see *United States Naval Institute Proceedings*, vols. 84, no. 12 (December 1958), pp. 121–122; 85, no. 10 (October 1959), pp. 100–101; and 86, no. 5 (May 1960), p. 101.

urgency that a program of widespread construction involving the time-consuming kind of labor required to produce permanent forts could be undertaken; and such a period first occurred following the War of 1812. There were, of course, advantages to masonry beyond that of resistance to natural erosion. Its extreme resistance to impact within certain limits, for example, was clearly demonstrated in an early trial at Castle Williams, where a solid shot fired from close range penetrated the nine-foot wall to a depth of only about two inches. It was in terms of design, however, that the general use of brick and stone was of the greatest significance, for these materials made possible the inclusion of the casemate emplacement as a universal feature of major works constructed during the post-1816 era. The resulting extension of the trend toward multiple tiers of armament, which in the United States had begun in 1807, brought to an all-time maximum the number of cannon per unit area of defensive front. This high density of heavy armament, together with the fact that Third System forts were for the most part considerably larger than those of previous periods, resulted in the greatest amassment of weapons ever achieved in harbor defense. At the extreme, certain works of this era were given an expanse of seaward front and a number of casemate levels which permitted more than one hundred guns to bear simultaneously on a single target.[46]

As a fundamental element in the military architecture of the early nineteenth century, the casemate emplacement became a major focus of inventive efforts both here and abroad, with the result that some of the most important advances to be made in seacoast fortification consisted of improvements in the sizes and shapes of embrasures. It was, of course, desirable for several reasons to diminish these gun openings to a minimum; but without some radical change in embrasure design, any decrease in size necessarily meant a corresponding reduction in the scope of movement of the armament within. The problem was complicated by the fact that the cannon themselves were gradually being made larger.

The best solution appears to have been achieved in the United States, where General J. G. Totten, the Army's Chief Engineer from 1838 to 1864, devoted much of his professional life to the refinement of casemate details. By utilizing certain embrasure configurations he succeeded in bringing the openings down to an area of less than ten square feet, one-fourth or one-fifth the size of those in many European forts as late as 1855. Moreover, his design allowed the guns to swivel laterally through sixty degrees while those in Europe were generally limited to about forty despite the greater dimensions of their embrasures.[47]

46. Fort Jefferson, Florida, the largest example, had pairs of adjacent faces with emplacements for about 125 guns.
47. Abbot, *Lectures*, pp. 139–140; Joseph G. Totten, *Report on the Effects of Firing*

In an effort to reduce the vulnerability of casemates even further and to provide the greatest possible protection for gunners, Totten in the early 1850s conducted what was probably the most complete and thoroughly controlled series of material resistance studies yet undertaken in connection with defensive construction. As a result of these experiments, for the first time anywhere in the world armor was introduced as a standard element of harbor defense structures when the embrasures of a number of Third System works were lined with iron "throats" made up of plates several inches thick (Figure 17). In addition, the casemates of subsequent works, as well as those of some already in existence, were provided with iron embrasure shutters two inches thick, which opened the moment a piece

FIGURE 17. Totten casemate embrasures at the west end of Fort Wool, Hampton Roads, Virginia. This unique work of elliptical plan, which was sited on an artificial shoal begun in 1818 and known as the Rip Raps, was to have been a three-tier fort of more than 200 guns. However, continued subsidence of the foundations under the weight of the structure's masonry led to prolonged suspensions of construction to allow the underlying rockfill to settle, and when the work was finally halted in 1870 it had progressed only to the level shown here. The iron embrasure throats and shutters are clearly visible, as is the staining of the stone caused by decades of rusting. Originally called Fort Calhoun, after John C. Calhoun, Monroe's Secretary of War, the work was renamed in 1862 to honor Major General John E. Wool, a leading commander of the Mexican War. Modern harbor defense batteries were located within the fort from about 1900 through World War II. (Photo by Lieutenant William R. Rodgers, 1969)

with Heavy Ordnance from Casemate Embrasures . . . and Against the Same Embrasures, Papers on Practical Engineering, no. 6 (Washington: Taylor and Maury, 1857), pp. 144ff.; J. G. Barnard, *The Dangers and Defences of New York* (New York: Van Nostrand, 1859), p. 39.

was fired, then slammed shut to shield the gun and its crew from grape shot and sharpshooters during preparations for the following round. The product of these innovations became internationally known as the Totten embrasure.[48]

Although the principal forts of the Third System shared the basic characterics discussed above, individual designs depended on several factors. The shape, the size, the armament, and the height of any given work were all affected by its remoteness from (or proximity to) a populated area, the nature of the surrounding topography, the size and importance of the channel it was designed to protect, the specific period during which its construction took place, and the state of development in various related aspects of technology, both of weaponry and of communications. Whether it was built of brick or stone depended on the region in which it was located, as did, to some extent, the specific type of stone used. Since construction covered a period of nearly fifty years and ranged from Maine to California, the variation among the forts was considerable.

For the most part these forts were polygonal in plan, some having as few as four faces while others had as many as seven. Perimeters varied from two or three hundred yards to well over a mile, and armament from fewer than fifty guns to about four hundred. In practically every instance one or more arched tiers of casemates extended the full length of each seaward front, and a roof tier of barbette emplacements normally surmounted each exterior wall (Figures 18 and 19). The structural materials were either brick or stone, though occasionally both; small amounts of earth were used to support sodding around the barbette emplacements. External walls varied in thickness but were generally of a minimum of about five feet around the embrasures. In most cases they were separated slightly from the piers and arches supporting the floor levels to avoid the problems resulting from unequal settling entailed in construction of such massive proportions.

Examples of almost every variety of design and stage of development during this long era may still be seen, for of the more than thirty Third System forts begun after 1816, nearly all remain in existence. Several have been partially obscured by the superimposition of more recent works, and the exterior walls of a few have been buried behind earthen slopes formed during or after the Civil War, when there was a return to the earthwork type of protective construction. Most, however, remain in essentially their original form, today constituting as a group the oldest surviving body of major military structures in the United States.

48. Abbot, *Lectures*, pp. 139–141; Barnard, *Dangers*, pp. 37–39; Totten, *Casemate Embrasures*, pp. 153–155; E. E. Winslow, *Lectures on Seacoast Defense*, U.S. Army Engineer School Occasional Papers, no. 35 (Washington: The Engineer School Press, 1909), p. 8.

FIGURE 18. Casemate tier of a Third System fort. This mode of construction and arrangement of armament was general among Third System forts, though structural materials and minor details varied. Every major fort had at least one such tier of emplacements, several had two, and some were designed with three. This drawing, done probably around 1875, shows the 10-inch Rodman guns that replaced the original 32- and 42-pounder armament during and shortly after the Civil War. (Photo, in author's collection, of drawing, probably mid 1870s)

Facing page, above

FIGURE 19. Barbette tier of a Third System fort. In addition to one, two, or three levels of casemated guns, pre-Civil War forts normally had roof batteries of heavy weapons along the seaward fronts and, in some cases, lighter armament facing landward. Shown here is a row of 8-inch shell guns, or columbiads, overlooking the entrance to San Francisco Bay from atop the fort at Fort Point (see Figure 30). (Photo by Edward Muybridge, courtesy San Francisco College for Women, about 1870)

Facing page, below

FIGURE 20. Cross section through the seaward front of a typical fort of the Third System with two casemate tiers. The guns on the lower levels are 42-pounders on pre-Civil War casemate carriages (see Figure 31). The roof armament is the Model 1844 columbiad on the wooden columbiad barbette carriage. (Drawing by author)

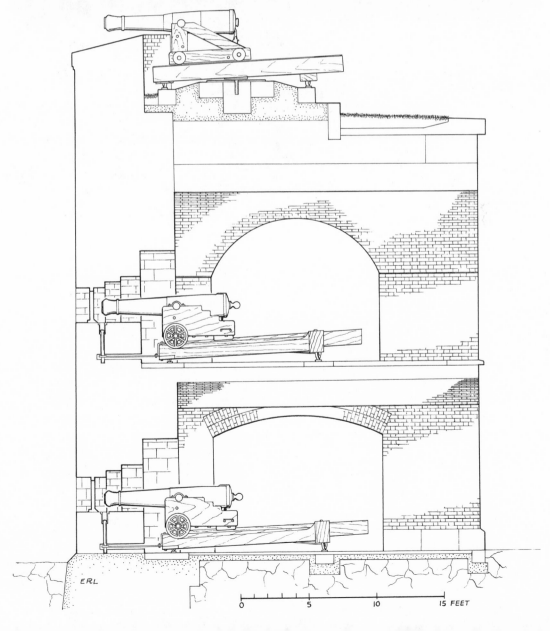

ERL

0   5   10   15 FEET

Figure 21. Fort Monroe, Virginia, begun in 1817 to command Hampton Roads, was the first work of the Third System planned from the ground up. It was also the most extensive in area of all pre-Civil War forts and was long thought to be the largest defensive structure in the world that did not enclose a civilian community. The work was designed by Simon Bernard as an irregular hexagon with a large bastion at each salient (i.e., at each intersection of major faces) and an additional bastion on the long southern front. Named for the fifth President, it was officially known until 1832 as Fortress Monroe (see footnote 49, page 52). The Army's first service school—the Artillery School of Practice—was founded here in 1824, and during the first half of the twentieth century its successor, the Coast Artillery School, made Fort Monroe the hub of harbor defense training, research, and development activities. It now serves as Headquarters, U.S. Continental Army Command (CONARC). (Photo, U.S. Army, early 1960s)

FIGURE 22. Fort Adams, near Newport, Rhode Island, was designed principally by Joseph G. Totten, a member of the original Bernard Board. Begun in 1824, it was constructed as an irregular and prominently bastioned pentagon with a single casemate tier except along the face fronting the main channel, where there was an additional level of casemates. The enclosed work shown to the left of the main fort was intended for landward defense. The name, Fort Adams, was carried over from the First System work on the same site, which had been named in honor of President John Adams on July 4, 1799. (Photo by author and D. P. Kirchner, 1966)

FIGURE 23. Fort Schuyler was begun on Throgs Neck in 1833 to guard the eastern (Long Island Sound) entrance to New York Harbor. This photo shows the reduced size and symmetrical form common among Third System forts constructed from about 1830 on. Also visible are three bastions of the later style, much diminished in size from those of Forts Monroe and Adams and of the earlier systems. The landward outwork, of the kind adjacent to several peninsular forts, was not a universal Third System feature. This fort was named for Major General Philip Schuyler of the Continental Army, and is now part of the New York State Maritime Academy reservation. (Photo by D. P. Kirchner, 1969)

Facing page, above

FIGURE 24. Named in honor of Brigadier General Casimir Pulaski, Continental Army, this work was begun in 1829 on Cockspur Island, Georgia, near the mouth of the Savannah River. Like Fort Sumter, which it resembled in plan, Fort Pulaski was to have an important place in the history of the Civil War. Occupied by state troops in January 1861, three months before the surrender of Fort Sumter, it was retaken fifteen months later by Federal forces after a long-range bombardment in which the southeast salient (nearest the camera in the photo above) was successfully breeched with relative ease by rifled artillery (see page 67). More than any other single event, this first major success in the use of rifled guns against a masonry defensive work spelled the end of the style of fortification represented by the Third System. Though badly damaged during the war and generally abandoned thereafter, Fort Pulaski has gradually been restored, largely during the 1930s by PWA funds and CCC labor, and is now a national monument. (Photo G-370, National Park Service, about 1950)

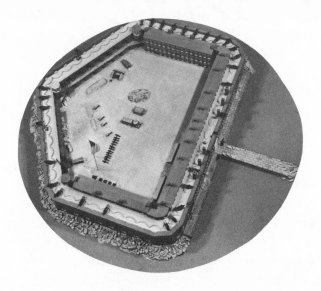

FIGURE 25. A National Park Service model of Fort Sumter, Charleston, South Carolina, shows the work as it appeared at the beginning of the Civil War, just prior to its bombardment. A multi-tiered fort of simple non-bastioned design, it was begun in 1829 and constructed in the form of a truncated hexagon. It was reduced largely to ruins during the Civil War, following which repairs were begun and gradually carried out until about 1885. In the late 1890s, a large part of the interior was filled in with earth and concrete as part of the emplacement of a pair of modern 12-inch rifled guns (see Figure 45). These remained in service until World War II, after which the fort became a unit of the National Park Service. It was named for Thomas Sumter, Brigadier General of the South Carolina Militia during the American Revolution. (Photo WASO-G-927, National Park Service)

The earliest forts of this era, aside from their more impressive scale, rather resembled the polygonal specimens of the preceding periods with regard to their large bastions and irregularity of plan. Both characteristics are well illustrated in Fort Monroe, Virginia,[49] and Fort Adams, Newport, Rhode Island, two extensive works that were both commenced prior to 1825 (Figures 21 and 22).

As the period proceeded, the construction of very large forts was generally given up, especially as the development of railroads made it possible to move large numbers of troops rapidly to the support of a permanently fortified position, and thereby reduced the need for huge works capable of sustaining prolonged sieges. Few really large works, in fact, were begun after about 1830, and these were in every case situated on islands or in other isolated circumstances. Two such works are illustrated on pages 55 (Figure 28) and 90 (Figure 44).

At the same time, the forts tended to become taller and more nearly regular in plan, as symmetrical works with additional tiers of casemates began to appear. Though many were still provided with bastions, a larger proportion of the principal seacoast armament (as opposed to the smaller guns used for flank defense of the faces) was concentrated in the major fronts, and the bastions were accordingly reduced in size. Fort Schuyler (Figure 23), begun in 1833 at the eastern entrance to New York Harbor, clearly exhibits these various developments—the reduced and symmetrical form, the double tier of casemates, and the diminished bastion.

The general plan most common for Third System forts, especially those begun after the mid-1820s, was based on the regular hexagon, a form dictated in part by the traversing limits of the casemate gun carriages and the size of the embrasures. Since these weapons were restricted to 60 degrees of lateral movement, adjacent fort fronts had to intersect at angles of at least 120 degrees if dead spaces (areas outside the arc of any gun's fire) were to be avoided within the target area.

The hexagonal form was often truncated on the land side, as in the system's two historically most important examples, both begun in 1829— Fort Pulaski (Figure 24), near Savannah, and Fort Sumter (Figure 25), in Charleston Harbor. Quite similar in general plan, these structures were devoid of projecting bastions on the seaward side, as were many of the works whose locations (either on marshlands, islands, or shoals) were such as to render them relatively secure from direct assault by land forces. Like Pulaski, some forts were provided with detached works to guard their landward approaches, and some were also surrounded by moats or ditches.

49. The name was changed from "Fortress" to "Fort" Monroe by Order No. 11, Headquarters of the Army, February 8, 1832. For Bernard's part in creating this work, see Arthur, *Fort Monroe,* p. 42; also, miscellaneous pamphlets in the series, "Tales of Old Fort Monroe," published by the Casemate Museum, Fort Monroe, Virginia.

The forts of this era were almost invariably built within a few feet of sea level to deny passage to ships that might otherwise slip past beneath the fire of guns on elevated sites, and to permit ricochet fire, a widely used technique of skipping cannonballs along the surface of the water, which to a large degree relieved gunners of having to determine target distances and required them only to point their guns in the right direction.

High densities of armament were, of course, attained with the multiple-tiered casemate design that masonry construction made possible. Only at certain positions (mainly on the South Atlantic and Gulf coasts) was such construction precluded by physical limitations, an instance of which arose during the planning of Fort Pulaski, originally intended to have two casemate tiers, when it was determined that the muddy local soil of Cockspur Island would not support the required weight of brick.[50]

A few of the later works on the most important harbors were in fact constructed with up to four tiers of armament. Two excellent examples (Figures 29 and 30) are Fort Richmond, New York, and Fort Winfield Scott, San Francisco, which remain standing today at opposite ends of the continent, coincidentally in the shadows of two of the world's greatest bridges. Both are well preserved owing largely to their presence on continuously active military posts.

During the same era, between 1816 and the Civil War, seacoast armament was also advanced in many important respects. The guns, like those of the previous periods, were basically smoothbore muzzle-loading cannon that fired spherical projectiles, either solid iron shot or, in some instances, explosive shell. Numerous improvements were made, however, especially after about 1840, with regard to size, power, and reliability against bursting, a not infrequent sort of accident at that time. Moreover, all heavy armament procured during these years was, for the first time, designed and manufactured exclusively in the United States.

At the close of the War of 1812, the heavy cannon in the American arsenal were limited to some five hundred 24- and 32-pounders, plus the few dozen 42- and 50-pounders at Castle Williams, all of which could not begin to meet even the relatively modest initial requirements of the program laid out by the Bernard Board. Many of the pieces were old, some were certainly of doubtful strength, and patterns varied widely. The production of a considerable number of new cannon was demanded, and type standardization—the corollary of such production—became a necessity.[51]

Thus, design of heavy armament in effect began anew in 1819, the year in which model designations first appear to have been used by the United

50. Lattimore, *Fort Pulaski*, p. 6.
51. *ASP, MA*, vols. 1, p. 821; 2, pp. 338, 511.

FIGURE 26. Fort Gorges on Hog Island Ledge, harbor of Portland, Maine. One of the last Third System forts to be commenced (in 1857), this work was never fully completed, nor was it garrisoned except by small caretaker detachments. Named for Sir Ferdinando Gorges, the English founder of the colony of Maine, this work is an excellent surviving example of the half dozen or so forts which, like Sumter and Carroll, were built on small, sometimes artificial, islands. (Photo by author and D. P. Kirchner, 1966)

FIGURE 27. Fort Carroll, a casemated work on Soller's Point Flats in the Patapsco River below Baltimore. Begun in 1847 and named for Charles Carroll, a signer of the Declaration of Independence, this was one of several Third System forts in whose construction Robert E. Lee had a part as a pre-Civil War military engineer. This vertical photo of the 1920s shows the emplacements for three batteries of modern rifled guns constructed atop the original fort shortly before 1900. These consisted of two 12-inch, two 5-inch, and two 3-inch pieces (clockwise, beginning lower right), all of which were removed after World War I when the fort was abandoned by the Army. (Photo 2795 AS, U.S. Army Air Service, about 1925)

FIGURE 28. Fort Jefferson on Garden Key, Dry Tortugas Islands, Florida. Though not as extensive in area as Fort Monroe, this enormous work seventy miles west of Key West was the largest of all Third System forts in terms of the armament for which it was designed, about 450 guns. Built to cover a strategic anchorage in the Gulf of Mexico, it was one of only three forts in the south to remain in Federal hands throughout the Civil War. It was never fully armed or even completed though construction proceeded well beyond the war and into the 1870s. During the postwar years the fort became a prison housing, among others, some of the alleged Lincoln assassination conspirators. In 1900 it was transferred to the Navy Department, was later made available to the Department of Agriculture, and finally became a national monument in 1935. (Photo 62-JB-226, National Park Service, 1962)

FIGURE 29. Fort Richmond on Staten Island was begun in 1847 at the west side of the Narrows to replace a semicircular fort of the same name which had been built by the State of New York during the War of 1812. The name came from Richmond County (which comprises Staten Island), but the four-tiered work was redesignated shortly after the Civil War to honor Brigadier General James S. Wadsworth, who had been killed in May 1864 during the Wilderness Campaign. When the entire reservation was designated Fort Wadsworth in 1902, the Third System fort was once again renamed, this time as Battery Weed, after Brigadier General Stephen H. Weed, U.S. Volunteers, who was killed at Gettysburg. As a result, the old structure is now known locally by as many as four different names, "Fort" Weed having been understandably added out of the confusion. (Photo 1036443, U.S. Navy, 1958)

FIGURE 30. Fort Winfield Scott, at the Presidio of San Francisco, was the only major Third System structure to be built on the Pacific coast. Begun in 1853, it was continuously armed from 1861 to about 1900, but again saw service in World War II, when light rapid-fire guns were mounted on its barbette tier to guard against penetration of the harbor entrance by small fast boats. An outstanding example of late Third System architecture, the work was threatened with demolition around 1930 to make way for the Golden Gate Bridge. The designer of the bridge, however, fortunately recognized the fort's historical and architectural value and spanned the work with an enormous steel arch, thus saving it from destruction. Originally known as the fort at Fort Point, then simply as Fort Point, the structure was officially named in 1882 in honor of Brevet Lieutenant General Winfield Scott, who commanded the U.S. Army from 1841 to 1861, longer than any other individual. During recent decades the name "Fort Point" has again come to be used for the old brick and granite work, while Fort Winfield Scott, or simply "Fort Scott" has by custom but without official basis come to refer to the entire western portion of the Presidio reservation. (Photo, courtesy Redwood Empire Association, early 1960s)

States Army. The old weapons, though they remained mounted in the existing forts, were in essence shelved so far as the ordnance standards or the fortification requirements were concerned.[52]

New 24-pounders, the largest cannon called for by the Board in its early plans, began to be manufactured in quantity and remained the heaviest guns under production in the United States until 1829. In that year, because of revisions in the plans concerning the harbor defense armament, the casting of 32-pounders began, and three years later 42-pounders were added.[53]

Practically no more 24-pounder guns were made for seacoast use beyond this time, though an entirely new weapon of the same bore was adopted for the local protection of seacoast forts. Known as the 24-pounder flank-defense howitzer, it was the first standard piece developed expressly to cover the exterior faces from casemates within the bastions, a function which had previously been performed by a variety of small cannon selected mainly on the basis of availability.

The period between 1840 and the beginning of the Civil War was one of considerable progress in that it witnessed the design of several new kinds of heavy guns, both in the United States and abroad. But while foreign ordnance specialists tended to spend much of this interval in what proved for the most part to be premature attempts to bring about radical improvements in artillery (for metallurgy and manufacturing techniques could not yet keep pace with invention), Americans working in the field of heavy armament, most notably the Army's George Bomford and Thomas Rodman and the Navy's John Dahlgren, used the same years to advance cast-iron smoothbore ordnance to its ultimate level of development.

One important change occurred shortly after 1840, when Bomford introduced a versatile new seacoast weapon of greater size and flexibility and substantially greater range than the standard 42- and 32-pounders. The ordinary function of these existing guns, to project solid shot against the hulls of ships, demanded of them the capacity to execute either direct flat-trajectory fire or ricochet fire, the latter necessarily from lower casemate or water battery positions very near sea level.[54] Because both types of shooting

52. J. Leander Bishop, *A History of American Manufactures from 1608 to 1860* (3 vols., orig. published in 1868, reprinted, New York: Augustus M. Kelley, 1966), vol. 3, p. 98; William E. Birkhimer, *Historical Sketch of the Organization, Administration, Materiel and Tactics of the Artillery, United States Army* (Washington: Chapman, 1884), p. 280; U.S. Army Ordnance Department, *Catalog of Ordnance and Ordnance Stores* (Washington: GPO, 1880), pp. 275, 296, 321.

53. Bishop, *American Manufactures,* p. 98, dates the adoption of the 32-pounders in 1829, the addition of the 42s "Three years afterward . . ." The *Ordnance Manual for the Use of Officers of the United States Army* (Washington: Gideon, 1841), p. 4, lists the model years, respectively, as 1829 and 1831; *ASP, MA* (vol. 4, p. 934) indicates that the first post-1819 order for 32-pounders was placed on May 15, 1828. The proposed use of 32s is suggested as early as 1823 or 1824 (e.g., *ASP, MA,* vol. 2, p. 623).

54. The term "water battery" was widely used in connection with seacoast defenses,

were done with the pieces pointed horizontally or with only slight inclination, the carriages had always been designed to allow at the most five or ten degrees of firing elevation.[55]

The new weapons, known as columbiads, supposedly after the Bomford pattern of the 1812 period (see footnote 34), were produced in both 10- and 8-inch calibers (equivalent, respectively, to 125- and 64-pounders under the old system of measurement) to fire either shot or shell at any angle between zero and nearly forty degrees. As a result of this elevation increase, the maximum range of shore guns was tripled in the American service, for the 10-inch model could exceed three miles, in contrast to the 42-pounder's maximum range of just over a mile (see Appendix B, page 142). Moreover, their ability to fire both solid and explosive projectiles permitted their employment in a wide variety of situations, as armament for low-level casemates, upper level barbette tiers, or batteries on elevated sites.[56]

A more fundamental advance in heavy ordnance, the most significant, in fact, to be made so far in the United States, grew out of attempts to solve the centuries-old problem of the structural unreliability of cannon, in particular the tendency, especially of large pieces, to burst during firing. Although the improved weapons which resulted from this advance belong historically to the period of the Civil War, the developments that produced them came about primarily in connection with work on seacoast armament between about 1845 and 1860. Two aspects of design and manufacture were involved—the external shape of cannon; and the manner in which they were cast.

For hundreds of years artillery materiel had been patterned in a complexity of curved, angular, and linear shapes interspersed with moldings and rings of various widths, knobs, and handles which, while supposedly contributing to overall strength, were in large part purely ornamental. Although some of this adornment had gradually disappeared over the centuries, largely at the whim of individual cannon founders, it was only in the 1850s that sound experimental evidence finally became available to

normally to refer to a battery of guns, often a battery exterior to a major fort, that was located near the water and very slightly above water level (see, for example, figs. 14 and 15). The expression was also used to refer, however, to all the guns of a fort facing toward the water, to distinguish them from those sited to cover the land approaches.

55. J. G. Benton, *A Course of Instruction in Ordnance and Gunnery* (New York: Van Nostrand, 1859), pp. 180–183; John Gibbon, *The Artillerist's Manual* (New York: Van Nostrand, 1860), p. 461.

56. Birkhimer, *Historical Sketch of the Artillery*, p. 283; E. R. Lewis, "The Ambiguous Columbiads," *Military Affairs*, vol. 28, no. 3 (Fall 1964), p. 116; Bishop, *American Manufactures*, p. 99. Gibbon (*Artillerist's Manual,* pp. 43–45) gives as the maximum ranges of the 32- and 42-pounders, 1922 and 1955 yards, respectively, both at 5° firing elevation; of the 8-inch columbiad, 4812 yards at 27°30′, and of the 10-inch columbiad, 5654 yards at 39°15′.

indicate not only that such ornamentation generally contributed nothing to strength, but that in certain respects it actually increased the likelihood of failure through bursting.[57]

One of the men involved in these studies was Thomas J. Rodman, an Army Ordnance officer who was to become famous for several important contributions in the fields of armament design, metallurgy, and explosives. In the 1850s he began to develop a new type of gun, entirely devoid of ornamentation, the shape of which was based on the distribution of gas pressures within the piece during firing. Its external contour was patterned upon a curve obtained from actual pressure measurements taken at various places along the bore of a test weapon, and it provided at any given point along the gun's length a thickness of metal proportional to the stress at that point (see Figure 34, page 64). The same general concept was embodied in a gun also developed prior to the Civil War by the Navy's John Dahlgren, but although his design and Rodman's had a superficial resemblance, they were far from identical.

Since the 1840s Rodman had been involved in studying other gun-strengthening factors, one of which proved to be more important than shape, and it was his work in connection with this that constituted his greatest contribution to the advancement of heavy armament in the United States. It had been determined that in the casting of large iron cannon the sequence of cooling and hardening, which began at the outer surface and progressed toward the interior, left the finished gun under a pattern of stress directed toward the exterior. Since the pressures associated with firing were also directed radially outward from the bore, the total stress at the moment of firing sometimes exceeded the gun's limit of strain and caused the weapon to burst.

Rodman's solution was to reverse the pattern of stresses accumulated in the course of cooling by solidifying his castings in the opposite direction, i.e., by circulating cold water through the hollow core of a casting while keeping the exterior heated, so that the hardening sequence was from the bore toward the outside. The net effect was that the firing of guns cooled in this manner actually reduced rather than increased the total stress on their metal.[58] This problem in the casting of iron had been negligible with regard to smaller weapons, such as those used in field artillery. But it

57. Alexander L. Holley, *A Treatise on Ordnance and Armor* (New York: Trubner & Co., 1865), pp. 106–107; Gibbon, *Artillerist's Manual*, p. 99; Report of Proceedings of a Board of Officers assembled in Washington, D. C., in Pursuance of General Orders, No. 20, Adjutant General's Office, July 2, 1838, RG 156 (Records of the Office of the Chief of Ordnance), NA.

58. Bishop, *American Manufactures,* pp. 99–101; Testimony of Brevet Brigadier General T. J. Rodman, January 25–27, 1869, before the Joint Committee on Ordnance (printed in S. Com. Rpt. 266, 40th Cong., 3d Sess.).

increased appreciably with the mass of iron involved, and until it was solved it effectively precluded the making of guns beyond a certain size. Under Rodman's system of casting, however, it became possible to produce one-piece iron guns in calibers as large as 15 and even 20 inches.[59]

The era of the Third System is the earliest from which positive information is available concerning the detailed nature of gun carriages, for these, like the guns, were standardized for the first time during this period.

Throughout the War of 1812 and for some years after, the design of seacoast carriages tended to follow the general pattern of French origin noted previously, though each was individually constructed to fit the emplacements of a particular fort. As in earlier times, carriages were made of wood and continued to suffer a problem that had always accompanied the use of such carriages, a marked tendency to decay under normal exposure to weather unless maintained rigorously. Because of this difficulty, forts had generally remained unarmed in peacetime, except for a few pieces mounted for drill purposes; carriages for the bulk of the armament were either stored under shelter or fabricated only as war threatened.

In order to meet this problem, a carriage made of cast iron began to be produced after 1819. Though no drawing or record survives to reveal its details, the nature of the new material itself leaves no doubt that the change necessarily involved a degree of uniformity beyond that previously followed in manufacture. Such carriages were made in limited numbers for about twenty years, but in 1839 new wooden models were adopted, and these were completely standardized in design shortly thereafter.[60]

The wooden seacoast carriages of the 1840s and 1850s were of three basic types, each of which was made in various sizes to accommodate different calibers of guns. One type was used in casemate emplacements and mounted either guns or columbiads (Figure 31). A second model was used with barbette-mounted guns (Figure 32), while columbiads in barbette installations were provided with still a third type of carriage (illustrated in Figures 19 and 20). The 24-pounder flank-defense howitzer had a special carriage of its own (Figure 33). The various wooden carriages of this period remained standard only until about the beginning of the Civil War, but because they could be fabricated quickly and inexpensively they continued to be manufactured throughout the war, especially in the South, and many remained in use for years after.

59. During the Civil War nearly three hundred 15-inch Rodman guns were made, as was a single 20-inch experimental piece (*Ord. Rpts. & Papers,* vol. 3, p. 288; Bishop, *American Manufactures,* p. 103). An additional 20-inch gun was cast for the Navy in the same period.

60. Birkhimer, *Historical Sketch of the Artillery,* p. 254; Stanley L. Falk, "Artillery for the Land Service: The Development of a System," *Military Affairs,* vol. 28, no. 3 (Fall 1964), pp. 103ff.

FIGURE 31. Restoration of a casemate emplacement at Fort Sumter. The carriage is a replica of the standard pre-Civil War wooden casemate type. As in all carriages of this era, the upper portion rolled back with the recoil of firing, allowing room for the reloading of the gun. The incline of the chassis rails along which it rolled helped to absorb the recoil energy. The gun is one of nearly two hundred 7-inch rifles produced during the war from existing 42-pounders of the 1841 model. During its conversion to a rifle, this piece was strengthened by the addition of a heavy band of iron which was shrunk over the breech end. The cascabel, the round knob found at the rear of old cannon, has been broken off this particular piece. (Photo WASO-B-773, National Park Service)

FIGURE 32. A pair of 1841 model seacoast guns on wooden barbette carriages overlook the Potomac about ten miles downriver from Washington, D. C. Carriages of this design were introduced into the American service around 1840 and were manufactured in large numbers until the Civil War. Recoil was absorbed by the slope of the chassis and by friction, and the large spoked wheel was used to return the upper carriage and gun to the firing position after reloading. Like many of the smoothbore cannon and most of the wooden carriages presently to be seen at various historic sites throughout the United States, these two pieces are replicas. They were made in the early 1960s and installed on the barbette tier of Fort Washington, Maryland, under the supervision of the National Park Service. (Photo 9231-H, by Abbie Rowe, courtesy National Park Service, 1965)

FIGURE 33. Seacoast guns were mounted on and within the external walls of forts defending the entrances to harbors and rivers. The 24-pounder flank-defense howitzers, designed and mounted to protect the fort itself, were placed on swiveling wooden carriages within the bastion casemates of pre-Civil War forts to provide a curtain of fire along the exterior faces and for some distance outward over the surrounding area. The gun in the photo below is located in the small bastion of Fort Pulaski that may be seen at the upper left corner of the fort in Figure 24. It points generally along the moat and overlooks the entire landward side of the work as far as the opposite bastion (the near left corner of the fort in Figure 24), where an identical weapon was mounted. (Photo, National Park Service, 1957)

FIGURE 34. A 15-inch Rodman gun mounted in the defenses of Washington, D. C., during the Civil War. Designed by Thomas J. Rodman in the years preceding the war and cast according to a technique developed by him, the design and method of manufacture marked the culmination of smoothbore ordnance and produced the largest, most powerful, and most reliable cast-iron guns ever to be made. Nearly three hundred 15-inch Rodmans were produced during the war, along with more than twelve hundred similar guns in 10- and 8-inch sizes. Some were installed in the permanent seacoast forts, but a great many were used in the defense of important inland positions. The temporary wartime emplacement shown here, one of the dozens of defensive works erected around the national capital, was known as Battery Rodgers, and was located in the southern part of Alexandria, Virginia, overlooking the Potomac. After 1865 practically all such works were demolished and their guns were moved to the coasts, where some remained in service until after 1900. (Photo 111-B-353 [Brady Collection], National Archives, about 1863)

In the mid-1850s iron—this time wrought iron—began to be reintroduced in connection with a pre-Civil War modification of the columbiad. And just prior to the war this finally became the standard material of American seacoast carriages, all future models of which were to be of wrought iron until the early 1890s.

Throughout most of the period between 1820 and 1850, the production of cannon had tended to lag behind the completion of new defensive works, but by the outbreak of hostilities in 1861 the store of heavy ordnance roughly approximated the existing fortification requirements. Because the forts were generally under-garrisoned and carriages were in short supply, however, relatively few guns were actually mounted. Many works, some of them in crucial locations, were seriously short of their designed armament on the eve of the war. Fort Pulaski, built for 146 pieces, had only 20 installed; Sumter had about 60 of its 135 in place. Moreover, there was practically no reserve of heavy cannon available to replace those that might be damaged in service or to arm the dozens of temporary works which were to be erected over the years to come.[61]

The critical problem, however, was fortunately averted by the perfection just prior to the war of the new weapon designed by and subsequently named for Thomas Rodman, which represented cast-iron smoothbore ordnance carried to its absolute practical limit. The largest piece, of 15-inch caliber (Figure 34), was easily the most powerful service cannon in the world, and it was quickly adopted as the new standard seacoast weapon along with 10- and 8-inch models of similar design. Produced in large numbers throughout the war (including a single experimental monster of 20-inch size), more than a thousand Rodman guns went to fill the gaps in the Union forts, not only on the harbors but in the interior as well; and hundreds remained to constitute the primary coast defense armament for an additional twenty years, beyond which some of them saw further service in emergency batteries during the Spanish-American War.[62]

61. Lattimore, *Fort Pulaski,* p. 10; Frank Barnes, *Fort Sumter National Monument, South Carolina* (National Park Service Historical Handbook Series Number 12, Washington: GPO, 1952), pp. 5, 9; Letter, H. K. Craig, Colonel of Ordnance, to Jefferson Davis, Secretary of War, February 2, 1856, on the inexpediency of mounting guns at ungarrisoned forts (in *Ord. Rpts. & Papers,* vol. 2, pp. 575–576).

62. The Rodman gun was adopted as the standard seacoast weapon on February 4, 1861 (*Ord. Rpts. & Papers,* vol. 2, p. 223). Following the war the 8- and 10-inch pieces were reduced to the category of "retained" ordnance, i.e., no longer standard but to be kept in service until replaced by standard weapons (Report, February 12, 1868, of the Ordnance Board convened by order of the Chief of Ordnance, December 17, 1867 [RG 156, NA]). The 15-inch gun remained standard into the 1880s. At the same time, around 1885 about two hundred of the retained 10-inch pieces were converted into 8-inch muzzle-loading rifles by sleeve insertions (*Ord. Rpts. & Papers,* vol. 3, p. 377). These, as well as the 15-inch smoothbores, continued in limited service for nearly two decades more, until about 1903.

The generation of defenses which began under Bernard was not, in the end, ready for war, certainly not for the sort of war that befell the nation in 1861. One contingency essentially unforeseen in long-term peacetime planning was the sudden seizure of these works by domestic forces. American military policy in general involved the assumption that there would always be time for mobilization. Thus the forts had been completed structurally, but left only partially armed and largely unmanned, with the expectation that a threat of war would never arise so suddenly as to deny the margin of time needed to bring them to a state of readiness.

The conditions that allowed all but three of the major works south of Hampton Roads to fall into Confederate hands early in 1861 were unrelated, however, to their intrinsic functional qualities.[63] In purely technical respects, the seacoast fortifications of the United States as of 1861 represented an impressive combination of design excellence, construction quality, and armament power that was probably unsurpassed anywhere in the world. When, within a few years, these same defenses became obsolete, this was due not to any inherent flaws but to a radical and largely unforeseeable advance in the ordnance with which they were faced.

Post-Civil War Interlude

It is difficult to describe concisely the magnitude or the character of the Civil War's influence on the nature of arms, for this conflict produced some of the most momentous technical changes in the history of warfare. With reference to the present topic, it may be said that the impressive and very costly masonry forts protecting the harbors of the United States were almost overnight and without exception relegated to obsolescence. Warships improved significantly in terms of both their offensive effectiveness and their defensive capacity. Steam was used extensively for the propulsion of naval vessels, freeing them from dependence on winds and greatly increasing their tactical mobility. At the same time, the shift from sails to steam lessened the exposure of their means of propulsion, while the application of iron armor further reduced their vulnerability to shore fire. More important to the developmental history of basic weaponry, however, was the unusually thorough trial of rifled artillery which this war provided, settling beyond question a number of issues that, to many professionals, had

63. Most of the southern works were occupied by state forces two or three months before the bombardment of Fort Sumter. The three forts which did not fall into Confederate hands were Taylor (Key West), Jefferson (Dry Tortugas), and Pickens (Pensacola), all in Florida.

at most been interesting but inconclusive speculations left over from the previous decade's Crimean War.

The invention of cannon during the fourteenth century had led to the end of vertical-walled fortification in land warfare. From that time, it had been accepted virtually as axiomatic that masonry must never be exposed to the fire of heavy guns on land. Nevertheless, stone and brick continued to be used in harbor defense construction for centuries, for the rule did not apply to seacoast forts.[64] This difference was due to the fact that while individual cannonballs had little damaging effect on masonry, siege guns on land could be directed with sufficient accuracy against a small area of a wall to breach it by repeated battering. On the other hand, smoothbore naval cannon fired from moving vessels with unsteady decks lacked the precision needed to shatter masonry in this cumulative fashion, and harbor defense works consequently remained relatively invulnerable.

The appearance of rifled guns, however, changed this situation entirely. Rifling—the spiral grooving of a weapon's bore to impart a stabilizing spin to its projectiles—had long been used to advantage with small arms, but its application to cannon had been brought to a reasonably workable level only in the decade or so preceding the Civil War, and it had not yet received a really intensive test. What rifling did was to make possible the in-flight stabilization of elongated (i.e., pointed) projectiles, and thus to open the way to the several advantages of such projectiles over the spherical cannonballs fired by smoothbores. These advantages stemmed mainly from the fact that an elongated projectile comprises a far greater mass than a sphere of identical diameter, but does not encounter a corresponding increase in air resistance during its flight. In other words, rifled guns could deliver against a given target much larger effective impact energies than smoothbores, at substantially increased ranges, and, in general, with greatly improved accuracy.

The introduction in large numbers of such artillery during the Civil War, most of it of a type designed by a former ordnance officer of the Army, Robert P. Parrott, soon furnished a clear demonstration that rifled cannon, even the fairly primitive muzzle-loading varieties of 1861–1865, were capable of accomplishing quickly and easily what smoothbores could achieve only after long, tedious bombardments—the reduction of vertical walls to rubble. Because of their heightened effectiveness, rifled guns could do significant damage even in single hits, and in this lay their historical triumph over masonry.

Faced with such weapons, both sides fairly early in the war discovered the superiority of defenses constructed of earth or sand, where a hole made

---

64. Abbot, *Lectures,* pp. 138–139.

by a projectile could be rapidly repaired by filling, while a hit on masonry let loose a hail of stone splinters and produced damage that was practically irreparable. The armies soon turned to the widespread use of sand bags and makeshift earthwork emplacements, frequently backed by timber. While several Third System forts were in fact completed in accordance with original plans at the more important harbors during the war years, the fortifications initiated after the beginning of hostilities and throughout the war were almost exclusively earthworks, erected in large numbers on inland rivers, around cities, and in several positions along the coast (see Figure 34).

By 1865 several European nations were already starting to respond to the technical lessons of the Civil War by drafting plans for the construction of entirely new, and extremely expensive, types of permanent harbor defenses armored with great masses of iron, thus beginning a trend in military architecture which was to continue well into the twentieth century, making use in its extreme instances of shore-mounted battleship turrets.[65]

The United States, however, was in no position to commence an extensive new system of harbor defenses. The planning engineers, mindful of the suddenness with which the existing (i.e., Third System) fortifications had been rendered obsolete, were reluctant for technical reasons to turn to elaborate works that might quickly become outmoded, as there was much to suggest—correctly, as events proved—a coming period of further rapid advances in artillery. Nor would such an undertaking if proposed have stood much chance of realization, for under the extreme postwar stress on reduced military spending, any appropriations large enough to be meaningful would also have been out of the question.[66]

Consequently, the two or three years after the end of the war saw construction activities limited to renewed work on certain still-unfinished Third System forts in an effort to provide at least some measure of added protection. At the same time, Army engineers were conducting experiments to determine the feasibility of facing the existing masonry works with iron armor, while the Ordnance Department was engaged in designing and testing rifled guns of increased size and power, tentatively planned for adoption for seacoast use by the early 1870s. The armor studies were largely inconclusive, though this means of preserving the utility of Third System

65. The first such installation ashore consisted of a heavy cylindrical turret of two 16-inch guns mounted by the British at Dover in the 1880s. During the twentieth century battleship turrets were installed at several positions in Europe and Asia, including Heligoland, Bergen (Norway), Toulon, Sebastopol, Tsushima, Tokyo Bay, and Pusan (Korea).

66. *ARCE,* 1870, H. Exec. Doc. 1, 41/3, p. 9 (Serial 1447).

forts would probably have been ruled out by reason of cost in any event.[67]

The work on armament appeared promising, however, and it was largely this area of development that determined the specific nature of the next generation of defenses. Because of their size, the projected new weapons could not be mounted in the masonry forts. They were to be equipped, moreover, with carriages that would permit them to be withdrawn below the parapet crest for loading and servicing, and so provide adequate protection even in a simple barbette arrangement.[68] Thus, the inability of masonry to withstand modern weapons, the postwar shortage of funds for military purposes, and the need for emplacements large enough to receive the new armament combined in the closing years of the decade to bring about a return to an inexpensive mode of permanent fortification in which earth once again became the principal substance of protection.

On the whole, the works of the post-Civil War period (see Figure 35) were not greatly dissimilar from the barbette batteries of earlier systems. Most of the differences lay in details such as improved magazine placement and better spacing between adjacent guns. Because the works were designed for larger weapons, they were of greater size than previous earthworks. They were also more substantial and durable; facings were of brick, gun platforms were of granite and concrete, and ammunition storage rooms were heavily protected by earth and concrete.[69] And, for the first time since the Revolutionary War, separate batteries were to serve as the primary elements of harbor defense rather than as accessories. Although this sacrificed the tremendous concentration of weapons represented by casemated forts, it nevertheless offered genuine tactical benefits, for defensive armament could be grouped in any number of comparatively inexpensive works distributed among sites of maximum advantage along harbor entrances where concealment and protection from attacking ships could easily be secured. Moreover, batteries could be made of almost any size to contain as many or as few guns as needed in a given position, and they could be built on practically any plan to conform to local topography.

A large number of such works was commenced about 1870 under a fairly extensive program that included other means of defense as well, such as large-caliber mortars, torpedos (i.e., mines), and channel obstructions. It was, however, to be among the most short-lived of all American harbor

67. *ARCE,* 1869, H. Exec. Doc. 1, 41/2, pp. 5–6 (Serial 1413). Before the Civil War Totten had suggested that, were it not for the cost, fort faces might be armored in their entirety with iron (*Casemate Embrasures,* 157).

68. *ARCE,* 1869, H. Exec. Doc. 41/2, p. 6 (Serial 1413); *ARCE,* 1870, H. Exec. Doc. 1, 41/3, p. 5 (Serial 1447); *ARCE,* 1874, H. Exec. Doc. 1, 43/2, p. 4 (Serial 1636); Report of the Board of Engineers on the Condition of the Fortifications, dated November 30, 1881 (RG 77, NA).

69. Battery construction plans, RG 77, NA, Cartographic Branch.

defense efforts. For a time battery construction proceeded rapidly, but because development of the new weapons progressed more slowly than anticipated, completed works had to be armed in most instances with existing smoothbores, generally 15-inch Rodmans. The guns and carriages still under study did not in fact go into production, nor were any steps taken to install mines or obstructions except on an experimental basis.

Within about five years fortification appropriations stopped, and construction came to a halt soon thereafter, at a time when most of the gun batteries were unfinished, many of those completed were still unarmed, and not more than one or two mortar batteries were even begun. In the absence of adequate garrisons, completed and partially completed works were generally abandoned except for some located in the immediate vicinity of older defenses.[70] Although small annual appropriations continued to be made for several years, the amounts were nothing more than token sums given nominally for maintenance. The deserted batteries were periodically inspected by caretakers, but neither funds nor labor was available to them for arresting the progressive deterioration that was to continue into the early 1890s. Third System forts, though patently outdated, and armed for the most part with smoothbore guns of Civil War or earlier vintage, continued to serve, of necessity, as major components of the nation's harbor defenses.[71]

This abortive program nevertheless marked a distinct turning point in American fortification practice, for the technical and tactical concepts on which it was based set a pattern that was to characterize all future harbor defense undertakings in the United States. Never again would forts be built in the storybook style as single structures housing large numbers of cannon. From this time on, a fort was a piece of real estate occupied by a number of dispersed individual batteries. Furthermore, the various items of armament intended for this project, though never in fact adopted, remained under constant development throughout the 1870s and 1880s, with the result that by about 1890 there became available greatly improved weapons around which was conceived the very advanced and extensive generation of defenses that followed.

70. *ARCE,* 1880, H. Exec. Doc. 1, 46/3, p. 16 (Serial 1953); Eugene Griffin, *Our Sea-Coast Defences,* Military Monographs No. 1 (New York: G. P. Putnam's Sons, 1885), p. 9.

71. Griffin, *Defences,* p. 9; *Ord. Rpts. & Papers,* vol. 3, pp. 310, 377. Civil War rifled Parrott guns in the large calibers suitable for seacoast service were few in number and had been found during the war to be highly unreliable in terms of their tendency to burst (S. Com. Rpt. 266, 40th Cong., 3d Sess., pp. 211ff. [Serial 1362]). Although the lighter, field-caliber Parrotts were excellent, dependable weapons, the heavier models were downgraded shortly after the war to "retained" status along with the 8- and 10-inch Rodmans (cf. fn. 62).

FIGURE 35. A pair of 10-inch Rodman guns in a harbor defense installation of the early 1870s. During a brief period not long after the Civil War, a number of new and relatively inexpensive barbette batteries of earth, brick, and concrete were begun to replace the forts of the Third System. This program was halted by lack of funds in the mid-1870s, long before most of the projected defenses were completed. The battery pictured above, at the Presidio of San Francisco, was to have comprised eight pairs of emplacements such as those shown, but only 4 of the 16 guns were ever mounted. The doorway at the right was the entrance to the ammunition magazine, which was covered by several feet of earth over concrete. (Photo by Granville Blick, courtesy Loretta Blick Thompson, about 1900)

FIGURE 36. The harbor defense construction begun after the Civil War marked the beginning of an entirely new trend in the positioning of seacoast fortifications. In contrast to the high concentrations of armament sought by designers of Third System forts, the new works were planned to be dispersed at the most tactically favorable locations permitted by the terrain and the extent of the available land. In some areas new tracts were acquired for battery sites, and in certain instances these acquisitions had profound long-term effects upon regional land use. A particularly clear example is to be found in the San Francisco area, where the entire northern shore of the harbor entrance (left foreground in the photo) was obtained in 1866 to provide sites for several new batteries. Most of this land is still in Federal hands and thus remains free of commercial and residential development despite its location in the midst of a region of mushrooming growth. Additional acquisitions for subsequent harbor defense programs contributed to the preservation of still other extensive tracts in and around San Francisco. In this view of the Golden Gate, "A" and "B" mark the two points at which all pre-Civil War armament was concentrated—Fort Point and Alcatraz Island—while the positions of the postwar batteries are indicated by arrows. (Photo, U.S. Naval Air Station, Alameda, 1956)

THE MODERN ERA:

Concrete, Steel, and Breech-Loading Rifles

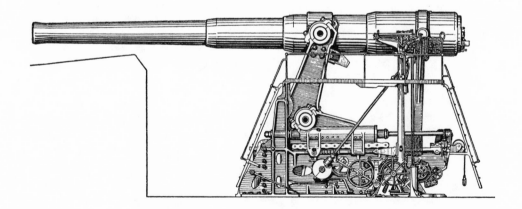

Endicott and Taft Periods

During the years following the termination of harbor defense construction in the mid-1870s, while the fortifications fell into disrepair and the defensive strength of the United States fell to perhaps its lowest point since 1812, several critical advances took place in the design and production of heavy ordnance. These developments, which revolutionized seacoast armament, involved the first large-scale use of steel for guns, the perfection of breech loading, and the introduction of far more effective propellants.

The substitution of steel for iron in gun manufacture became possible only with the maturing of the domestic metals industry in the years of its rapid growth after 1865. Availability of steel and the capacity of the industry to produce increasingly massive forgings at last permitted the large-scale practical achievement of a weaponry form conceived many years earlier, the compound gun. The fabrication of a cannon in accordance with this concept, which involved building up the barrel by the successive shrinking on of many separate concentric tube members rather than by machining it from a single, homogeneous casting, had first been attempted seriously in the years before the Civil War, mainly in England; but the technology of that period had precluded all but the most tentative applications of the idea. Not until the late 1880s did the combined availability of good quality steel in large amounts, industrial facilities for producing heavy forgings, and machining techniques able to meet the required standards of precision make it possible to produce substantial numbers of these lighter, stronger, longer, and, hence, more powerful weapons.[72]

Breech-loading, the second important development, had been employed with varying success in light cannon since before the Civil War, and intermittently for centuries before that. Workable breech-loading for heavy cannon, long sought because of its many obvious advantages, both technical and tactical, had eluded military and naval ordnance designers because of the difficulty of achieving a breech mechanism that could repeatedly withstand the extreme temperature of firing and contain (in part by finely fitted metal-to-metal surfaces) the tremendous gas pressures thus generated, and yet be opened and closed rapidly. Not until the late nineteenth century did the manufacturing arts reach the level required to produce the large, heavy, and extremely well machined blocks and recesses that successful breech-loading demanded.[73]

72. Holley, *Ordnance and Armor*, pp. 837–874; Lawrence L. Bruff, *A Text-Book of Ordnance and Gunnery Prepared for the Use of Cadets of the U.S. Military Academy* (New York: John Wiley, 1896), chapter 3.
73. Breech-loading had been used during the early centuries of the history of artillery but given up because no practical means of obturation (prevention of the escape of

75

This development permitted the first really complete utilization of rifling, which made possible the employment of far more efficient and effective projectiles. Breech-loading also made it possible to mount guns on entirely new types of carriages and within emplacements of a design that allowed the guns to be lowered by their own firing recoil energy to positions behind the parapets where they could be loaded in comparative safety. These advances, in turn, both accelerated the rate of operation and removed the crews from the enemy's view and fire.[74]

And finally, the centuries-old use of gunpowder and its derivatives began to give way before new propellants whose burning properties were such as to produce substantial increases in muzzle velocities and yet to reduce the mechanical stresses on guns. With these new powders, it became possible to improve the precision with which burning rates could be controlled (mainly by variation in grain size), and thus to maintain the production of gases within the bore of a gun over a predictable period. Unlike the older gunpowders, which, regardless of granular texture, were consumed almost instantaneously, usually while the projectile was still well within the bore, the new, relatively slow-burning substances could be regulated to continue the exertion of constructive accelerative force upon the projectile throughout its entire progress along the length of the gun. This property of the modern propellants, in order to be most fully exploited, demanded the substantial lengthening of gun tubes; and the metallurgical and technological advances noted above had already made this increase in length possible.

The magnitude of the effect on heavy ordnance of this combination of developments can hardly be exaggerated, for together they represented within the space of a few decades the greatest advance to be made in artillery between its invention in the fourteenth century and the appearance of the nuclear projectile in the mid-twentieth. Compared to the best of the smoothbore muzzle-loading cannon of the post-Civil War period, the new weapons which began to emerge from the developmental stage around 1890 could fire projectiles that, caliber for caliber, were four times as heavy to effective ranges two to three times as great; and they could do so with remarkably increased armor-penetration ability and accuracy.[75]

---

gas) had been worked out. The development of new breech-closing devices, as of the time of the Civil War, is treated in Holley, *Ordnance and Armor*, pp. 580ff. For more modern breech systems, see Bruff, *Ordnance and Gunnery*, chapter 3.

74. Earlier American attempts to devise disappearing carriages (about 1870, as mentioned on p. 69) are illustrated and described in the report of the Chief of Ordnance for the fiscal year ended June 30, 1873 (printed as H. Exec. Doc. 1, part 2, vol. 3, 43d Cong., 1st Sess. [Serial 1599], pp. 459–479). For the type of carriage adopted during the Endicott period, see Bruff, *Ordnance and Gunnery*, pp. 430ff.

75. The 10-inch Rodman (prior to its conversion as a rifle—see fn. 62) had a maximum range of about 4,000 yards with a 123-pound shot; the 10-inch rifled gun of 1890 had a range of about 12,300 yards with a 604-pound projectile.

While this generation of armament was still in the making, foreign progress in naval guns and vessels intensified the alarms which had been sounded since the cessation of harbor defense appropriations in 1875. Much of the public, a sizable group in Congress, and most officers of the Army and Navy were becoming increasingly concerned over the condition into which the fortifications had been allowed to deteriorate.[76]

In 1885, therefore, President Cleveland assembled a special Board headed by his first Secretary of War, William C. Endicott, to review the entire coast defense situation and to submit recommendations for a program based upon the newly developing weapons. This joint Army-Navy-civilian group, charged with the most comprehensive task of any such body since the time of Bernard, conducted an extensive study of the whole subject of fortification, types of armament, and protective materials.[77]

The program presented by the Endicott Board early in 1886 called for an enormous number of defensive works, including many with armored turrets and casemates, to be armed with weapons of unprecedented size and firepower. In addition to these fortifications, which were to be built at 26 coastal localities and 3 on the Great Lakes, it also provided for floating batteries, torpedo boats, and submarine mines.[78] In terms of the cost estimate alone, the overall proposal was grossly unrealistic. Moreover, the detailed provisions concerning the types and quantities of weapons, drafted while the new ordnance was still at a fairly early stage of development, were necessarily set forth long before precise information was available regarding the actual performance of the production models.

Thus, because of the unrealistic scope of the original plan, but also because the unexpectedly high performance of the new armament, once it appeared, made it possible to reduce the number of weapons required, the construction program begun in the early 1890s was marked by a series of reductions as the number of installations fell further and further below that envisioned by the Board. Against an original projecion of some thirteen hundred guns and mortars of 8-inch caliber and larger, fewer than seven hundred were actually installed.[79] The Board's report nevertheless formed the basic framework around which a new and completely modern generation of seacoast defenses took shape during the Spanish-American War

76. See, e.g., Griffin, *Defences; ARCE,* 1880, H. Exec. Doc. 1, 46/3, pp. 4ff. (Serial 1953); *ARCE,* 1881, H. Exec. Doc. 1, 47/1, pp. 4ff. (Serial 2011); *ARCE,* 1882, H. Exec. Doc. 1, 47/2, pp. 4ff. (Serial 2092).

77. H. Exec. Doc. 49, 49th Cong., 1st Sess. (Serials 2395, 2396), report dated January 23, 1886 [hereafter cited as *Endicott Board Report*].

78. Ibid., pp. 8, 24, 25.

79. The total estimate was $126,377,800 (*Endicott Board Report,* p. 28). A close approximation of the actual installations by caliber is given in *ARCE,* 1908, H. Doc. 1052, 60/2, p. 11 (Serial 5431).

and well into the first decade of the twentieth century. In this period, the harbors of the United States came once again to be protected by a vast body of fortifications, almost all of which, except for their armament, remain in existence to the present day.

The most evident change in the physical nature of harbor defenses involved the shift in emphasis from fortification structures toward the weapons contained therein. This shift was reflected in the character of the new gun emplacements which, though massive and costly, were relatively simple in form. In sharp contrast with the stark, vertical-walled forts of the Third System, the new works of reinforced concrete were de-emphasized by being designed to blend, so far as possible, into the surrounding landscape.

At the same time the new armament, aside from its greatly increased power and effectiveness, was far more complex than that of previous eras. In the 1850s heavy cannon had generally been turned out in a matter of days, but by 1900, several months could be consumed in the forging, machining, and painstaking inspection and measurement that went into assembling the built-up tube and breech mechanism of a single gun. And, over this same interval, the relative increase in cost and labor was even greater with respect to carriage production.[80]

The extent of this reversal in emphasis upon the major components of fortifications—weaponry and structures—is revealed by the percentage of harbor defense expenditures represented by each during the two periods. Prior to the Civil War the armament costs rarely amounted to even one-sixth of the total spent on any fort and were often less than one-tenth; on the other hand, in the 1890s the guns and carriages almost invariably represented half and sometimes as much as three-fourths the overall cost.[81]

In addition to its technical complexity, the new armament was characterized by a high degree of diversity in accordance with a newly emerging va-

80. For figures on the rate of mid-nineteenth-century cannon production, see, for example, Report of the Joint Committee on the Conduct of the War (Heavy Ordnance), printed in S. Rpt. 142, part 2, 38th Cong., 2d Sess., pp. 17ff. (Serial 1213). For figures for the period around 1900, see, for example, Chief of Ordnance reports throughout the 1890s concerning the progress of the one-hundred-gun contract with Bethlehem Steel, which was made in late 1891 and which was only 83 percent complete as of June 30, 1902 (Twelfth Report of the Board of Ordnance and Fortification, printed in H. Doc. 2, 57th Cong., 2d Sess. [Serial 4449]). Prior to about 1890 the cost of a carriage was typically about a third that of its gun; from that time on, the costs were roughly equal (e.g., the Model 1895 12-inch gun cost about $45,000, its carriage about $46,000).

81. Seventeen Third System forts costing a total of some $14 million were designed for armament having an overall cost of about $2.33 million, which included one hundred rounds of ammunition per gun (computed from various pre-Civil War sources); in 1900 a battery structure for two 12-inch disappearing guns cost roughly $100,000, while the two guns and carriages represented a total of approximately $180,000 without ammunition.

riety of harbor defense techniques. Along with the major-caliber seacoast weapons—the heavy guns emplaced to engage or repel similarly armed ships—the defenses included large numbers of mortars, as well as light-caliber rapid-fire guns sited to cover the fields of electrically controlled submarine mines which were to be installed as components of the total system.

The major armament of the Endicott era consisted of guns of 8-, 10-, and 12-inch caliber, the largest having a useful range of seven to eight miles with a 1,000-pound projectile. These were all flat-trajectory weapons whose firing angles, though limited to about fifteen degrees of elevation, gave them sufficient range to match or outshoot the guns of contemporary battleships. The great majority were mounted on the ingenious disappearing-type carriage which (as noted on page 76) utilized the energy of recoil to lower the gun within the emplacement, where it could remain for service and loading, concealed and protected from enemy fire until raised for the next shot. Mounted in massive emplacements whose crests were at ground level and whose concrete frontal walls were as much as twenty feet thick behind thirty or more additional feet of earth,[82] such armament was all but invisible and invulnerable from the seaward direction (Figure 37).

A few of the major-caliber weapons, particularly those sited at some height above the water (where they were safe from the low-angle fire to which naval vessels were at this time restricted), were mounted on a new type of barbette carriage, a greatly advanced outgrowth of the variety used throughout the nineteenth century (Figure 38). In both kinds of installations, disappearing and barbette, the ammunition magazines were located immediately adjacent to the gun emplacements, but at a level several feet lower, and roofed by a minimum of about twelve feet of reinforced concrete. The projectiles, weighing up to half a ton, were transported upward to the gun platform by a mechanical hoist resembling a dumbwaiter, then moved to the guns by hand trucks.

Roughly three hundred heavy guns were installed around continental harbors during the Endicott period, in batteries of from two to four weapons each, though in certain rare instances as many as six or seven pieces were grouped together in a continuous row of emplacements. Almost all the battery structures of this era may still be seen, usually on the seaward sides of former harbor defense reservations, many of which remain in military hands.

The second class of heavy armament during these years consisted of 12-inch mortars, stubby weapons installed in units of eight or sixteen, which were fired simultaneously to throw their 700-pound projectiles in high arcs to descend almost vertically in a shotgun-like pattern on the lightly armored decks of ships. The pieces were clustered in groups of four within square, pit-like emplacements, normally behind small hills or high artificial parapets

82. Battery construction plans, RG 77, NA, Cartographic Branch.

FIGURE 37. One of the most familiar technical features of the sea-coast fortifications built by the United States during the Endicott era was the disappearing carriage, on which some 270 guns of 8-, 10-, and 12-inch caliber were mounted. Though invented in Europe, this type of carriage was most highly perfected by two American ordnance officers, Adelbert R. Buffington and William Crozier, whose design was based on a counterweight principle rather than the trouble-some hydropneumatic system used in the original and many later European models. The Buffington-Crozier carriage consisted essentially of a pair of massive lever arms to support the gun tube. Upon firing, the tube and the upper end of the arms were carried to the rear and downward by recoil energy, which at the same time raised a heavy lead counterweight attached to the opposite end of the arms. Shown above an instant after firing is a 10-inch gun that has recoiled about one-fourth of the way rearward and down toward its loading position where, concealed from enemy sights and protected by earth and concrete against direct fire, it will be prepared for the next round. One great advantage of the Buffington-Crozier design was that, regardless of the angle at which the gun was fired, it always recoiled to the same position with respect to the concrete pavement behind the carriage. This made it possible to load the weapon directly from the wheeled shot trucks on which ammunition was brought from the magazines, and to dispense with the intermediate steps of ammunition handling required with other types of carriages. As a result, guns mounted in this fashion could be fired at very high rates —in tests with crack crews as fast as two rounds per minute. The gun in the loading position (facing, top) is about to be raised for the next round. A latch will be tripped to release the 55-ton lead weight, hanging in a well directly below the carriage, that will bring the gun back to its firing position. Both these photos were taken during target practice at Battery David Russell, Oregon, near the mouth of the Columbia River. This battery on the Fort Stevens reservation was constructed shortly after 1900 and named for Brevet Major General D. A. Russell, who was killed in action at Opequan, Virginia, on September 19, 1864. (Photos, from Marshall Hanft Collection, about 1936)

FIGURE 38. A 12-inch gun on a barbette carriage at Battery Godfrey, Presidio of San Francisco. The barbette carriages of the Endicott period did not offer the degree of protection provided by the disappearing type, nor could their guns be fired as rapidly, but they were considerably less expensive to manufacture. Adopted for service in 1892, such carriages were produced in relatively small numbers before the disappearing type was fully perfected. Altogether, fewer than fifty were installed with guns of 8-inch caliber and larger, though greatly improved barbette carriages of quite different design again came into service shortly after World War I (see Figures 55–57). The battery pictured below was completed in 1896 and consisted of three guns, the middle of which is shown firing during a target practice in July 1912. It was named for Captain George J. Godfrey, 22nd U.S. Infantry, who was killed on June 3, 1899, at San Miguel de Mayumo in the Philippine Islands. (Photo, courtesy Colonel E. L. Macaulay, 1912)

FIGURE 39. Battery Selfridge at Fort Kamehameha, near the entrance to Pearl Harbor. One of the last 12-inch disappearing gun batteries to be commenced (in 1907), this work was fairly typical of heavy-caliber batteries of the Endicott period, though the distance between its guns was somewhat greater than average for such batteries. The left gun is shown in the firing position, while that on the right has been lowered to the loading position. In the foreground may be seen a 12-inch railway mortar of the post-World War I period (see Figure 51). The fort, just east of the channel entrance to Pearl Harbor, was named for Kamehameha I, first king of the Hawaiian Islands, who died in 1819. The battery was named in honor of First Lieutenant Thomas E. Selfridge, a West Point classmate of Douglas MacArthur, who was killed at Fort Myer, Virginia, in 1908 during early tests of aircraft. (Photo 38-FCD-60, in the records of the Chief of Naval Operations, National Archives, about 1924)

that shielded them against direct naval fire; and two or four such pits in proximity constituted a mortar battery of up to sixteen weapons.

Long used in both coastal defense and siege warfare, mortars had previously been included in small numbers within the seacoast armament, and a few isolated pieces were usually to be found in most pre-Civil War forts. Only in the 1870s, however, was the first serious thought given to their installation in groups, when plans were prepared for mortar batteries to be located near New York and on the Delaware River. But it was not until twenty years later, after much additional technical and tactical development, that this type of weapon actually began to be incorporated into overall harbor defense thinking in accordance with a thoroughly formulated, if not yet empirically tested doctrine of employment. Ultimately, in the years after 1890, nearly four hundred 12-inch mortars came to be included in the fortifications of the United States.[83]

The projected laying of submarine mines within harbor entrances, and the need for such minefields to be covered against penetration by light sweeping craft or fast, shallow-draft vessels produced still a third class of armament during this period, an entire family of small guns which could be pointed, loaded, and fired very rapidly.

These weapons, of five different calibers from 3- to 6-inch, used ammunition light enough to be handled manually and could therefore be fired at service rates of 5 to 15 rounds per minute. Most of them were mounted behind steel shields on pedestal carriages of simple design, set in rather plain concrete emplacements with low surrounding parapets and adjacent protected magazines. The general arrangement of the rapid-fire batteries (of from two to six weapons each) somewhat resembled in miniature that of the barbette-mounted major-caliber guns. Though large numbers of this class of armament were not expressly proposed by the Endicott Board, project revisions led to the emplacement of over five hundred of these light pieces during the dozen years beginning about 1896.[84]

The defense of harbors by conventional fortifications had long been augmented by the use of channel obstructions designed either to preclude passage entirely or to force vessels to reduce their speed and thus to remain for a longer period of time within the fields of fire of shore-mounted guns. Until well into the nineteenth century chains or other kinds of barriers were often extended across harbor or river entrances, while in the twentieth the same general idea took the form of submarine nets. A related and more effective device was the underwater mine, which not only discouraged or impeded the

83. *ARCE*, 1872, H. Exec. Doc. 1, 42/3, p. 24 (Serial 1559). The *Endicott Board Report* recommended a total of 724 mortars (p. 24), but the actual number installed was 376 (*ARCE*, 1908, H. Doc. 1052, 60/2, p. 11 [Serial 5431]).

84. *ARCE*, 1909, H. Doc. 111, 61/2, pp. 11–12 (Serial 5726).

FIGURE 40. Mortar batteries normally consisted of two or four deep, pit-like emplacements, each of which originally had four mortars arranged in a square. In the first of these World War I photos (A), showing half of a two-pit battery at Key West, Florida, four mortars are about to be fired; they have been loaded and final aiming adjustments are being made. Immediately after firing (B), the weapons are lowered to zero elevation for reloading and the four crews of nearly a dozen men each rush forward to begin preparations for the next salvo (C). The final photo (D) shows the two rear mortars already loaded, while the detachments for the two in front are still loading and seemingly getting in each others' way. The forward pieces were normally the least accessible and most distant from the magazine and therefore took longest to load. Since none of the mortars in the pit could be fired until the area was cleared of extra personnel and loading equipment, the rate of fire was held to the speed with which the weapons at the front could be loaded. Although crews were highly drilled and could handle the 700-pound projectiles with remarkable speed, the congestion within the confined space during the loading operation did little to increase the effective rate of fire. A few of the later four-mortar pits were more spaciously designed, but as experience and improved techniques led to greater accuracy in firing, drills and target practices gradually began to be conducted with only two mortars of each pit, ordinarily the rear pair. As a result, rates of fire increased appreciably without a corresponding loss in effectiveness, and manning requirements were reduced. In most batteries the two forward weapons were removed, many of them to be mounted on railway carriages during World War I for use overseas (see Figure 51), and new batteries were designed for two mortars per pit (see Figure 65). (Photos A, C, and D, respectively, 111-SC-6754, -6752, and -6740, U.S. Army Signal Corps, in the National Archives; Photo B, author's collection; all 1918)

B

C

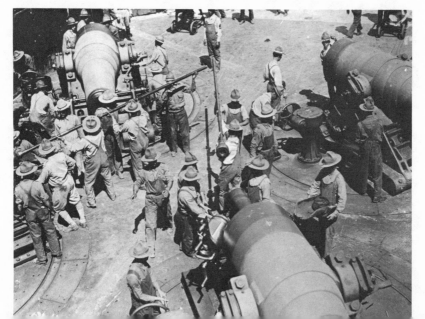

D

FIGURE 41. A fast camera catches a pair of 700-pound projectiles just fired from the two forward mortars in the "A" pit of Battery Anderson, Fort Monroe. Used for the training of personnel attending the Coast Artillery School, this battery continued in service until World War II, when it was deactivated along with all other remaining mortar batteries in the continental United States. It was named in honor of Brigadier General Robert Anderson who, as a major, commanded Fort Sumter at the time of its bombardment on April 12, 1861. (Photo 111-SC-55956, U.S. Army Signal Corps, in the National Archives, 1918)

Facing page, below

FIGURE 42. The light armament installed in the harbor defenses around 1900 comprised a large variety of weapons. With the exception of certain 6-inch models mounted on disappearing carriages, these rapid-fire guns all had shielded pedestal carriages generally similar to the 6-inch Model 1900 shown here. After World War I the War Department moved to reduce the large numbers of types and calibers, and about ten separate models, a total of nearly 300 pieces, were declared obsolete and scrapped. Included were all 5-, 4.7-, and 4-inch guns and carriages as well as some of the 6-inch disappearing and 3-inch pedestal weapons. Of the types retained, most were subsequently scrapped during World War II, though the Model 1900 continued in service until 1948. (Photo 165-WW-386D-1, in the records of the War Department General Staff, National Archives, about 1920)

Below

FIGURE 43. A total of more than 250 3-inch guns were installed in harbor defenses throughout the continental United States, Hawaii, and the Philippines. Over a hundred of these were of the Model 1898, four of which are shown below, emplaced in Battery Irwin at Fort Monroe. Along with most other rapid-fire weapons, the Model 1898 remained in service only until 1920 when it was classed as obsolete and removed from all such installations. Two of the emplacements of Battery Irwin were re-armed around the end of World War II with a pair of 3-inch guns of a later model, which escaped the general scrapping of seacoast armament in the late 1940s and are presently among the very few fixed weapons from the Endicott or later periods still in existence. This battery was named for First Lieutenant Douglas S. Irwin, 3rd U.S. Infantry, who was killed in action at Monterrey, Mexico, on September 21, 1846. (Photo 111-SC-9801, U.S. Army Signal Corps, in the National Archives, 1918)

entry of enemy ships, as did the passive obstructions, but could destroy them as well.

Many famous names were associated with the development of underwater mines, including those of David Bushnell, Robert Fulton, and Samuel Colt. Prior to 1860, such explosive devices (known until the early twentieth century as "torpedos") had already begun to fall into two major classes, depending on the manner in which they were detonated.[85] Contact or automatic types were made to explode by means of a trip wire or by impact, when hit, for example, by a passing vessel. Controlled mines, on the other hand, remained inert until exploded electrically, ordinarily from a position ashore to which they were connected by wire. It was on the latter type, especially adaptable to the defense of friendly channels, where it posed no danger to ordinary ship traffic, that the Army focused its attention shortly after the Civil War. Plans were made to include such devices in the project of the 1870s, but this program ended before any mines were installed, except on an experimental basis. Development continued throughout the ensuing years, however, and controlled minefields became an important component of the Endicott period defenses and of every other harbor defense project from that time on.[86]

Unlike gun and mortar batteries, however, mines were not permanently installed to remain in place for long intervals of time, but were stored ashore locally with their miles of control cable so that they could be planted rapidly in the event of an emergency. Each harbor having a projected underwater defense system was assigned a special mine-laying vessel; other elements of the system, such as fire-control stations, mine and cable storage facilities, and loading wharves, were constructed and maintained ashore. Normal peacetime activities were thus devoted to practice in planting and retrieving mines

85. The terms "mine" and "torpedo" were at times used interchangeably, though the former was, strictly speaking, an underground explosive charge usually placed to breach the exterior wall of a fort, while the latter was originally an explosive device for use under or on the surface of the water, usually anchored at a given place. When "torpedo" began to be applied around 1900 to the mobile, self-propelled devices still known by this name, the term "mine" was broadened to include stationary underwater or surface devices, as well as those used in land warfare.

86. *ARCE*, 1872, H. Exec. Doc. 1, 42/3, p. 25 (Serial 1559); *ARCE*, 1873, H. Exec. Doc. 1, 43/1, p. 25 (Serial 1598); *ARCE*, 1889, H. Exec. Doc. 1, 51/1, p. 7 (Serial 2716); *ARCE*, 1898, H. Doc. 2, 55/3, p. 12 (Serial 3746). Less has been published on the Army's submarine mining activities than on any other aspect of harbor defense. Brief general histories, however, are contained in Winslow, *Lectures*, pp. 118–147; Paul D. Bunker, "The Mine Defense of Harbors: Its History, Principles, Relation to the Other Elements of Defense, and Tactical Employment," *Journal of the United States Artillery*, vol. 41, no. 2 (March-April 1914), pp. 129–170; and Herbert C. Reuter, "A Summary of Historical Information Pertaining to Controlled Submarine Mining," prepared at the Submarine Mine Depot, Fort Monroe, Va., dated September 5, 1949. This topic is also mentioned briefly in two works devoted primarily to mining activities of the Navy, Arnold S. Lott, *Most Dangerous Sea* (Annapolis: United States Naval Institute, 1959), and Robert C. Duncan, *America's Use of Sea Mines* (Washington: GPO, 1962).

and to the constant development of materiel, such as electrical cable of improved durability and reliability. Not until World War II were the fortified harbors as a group finally mined, the Army's controlled fields in some cases being supplemented by groups of contact mines laid by the Navy.[87]

The entire program that began in the 1890s was characterized by the physical dispersion of armament elements into widely separated gun and mortar batteries, and this made necessary the acquisition of numerous new military reservations for weapon sites. Because of the sharp increase in gun power over that of the previous era, the positions were usually located, where land was available, in a seaward direction from the older works. When more favorably sited tracts could not be obtained, the new armament in some cases had to be installed within and on top of existing Third System forts. Examples of this form of battery placement may still be seen at such Atlantic and Gulf coast locations as Fort Warren in Boston Harbor; Fort Delaware on Pea Patch Island; Fort Sumter in Charleston Harbor; and Forts Morgan and Gaines, both near Mobile, Alabama. More often, however, the new batteries were simply constructed adjacent to, and outside of existing works in an arrangement that can be seen in practically any of the older major coastal forts along the Atlantic.

In 1905, President Roosevelt convened a group similar to the Endicott Board, this one headed by Secretary of War William Howard Taft. Its function was to review the earlier Board's program and bring it up to date, for in the twenty-year interval a number of developments had taken place that required incorporation into the harbor defense system. Some were purely technical; but during this period the United States had also secured several new territories, certain of which clearly required fortification.[88]

The major technical changes brought about by the Taft Board's recommendations were not so much in armament or fortification structures as in accessory harbor defense equipment. While it proposed few if any entirely new kinds of equipment, the Board's report did have the effect of accelerating the installation of many features which had been projected by the Endicott Board, but which had been neither fully developed until around 1900 nor yet installed except in limited numbers. Among these were batteries of searchlights for the nighttime illumination of harbor entrances, general electrification of all aspects of harbor defense (including such things

87. Various annual reports of the Chief of Engineers and the Chief of Coast Artillery, 1898–1940; Reuter, "Submarine Mining," pp. 4ff.; Conn et al., *Guarding the United States,* pp. 50–51; Duncan, *Sea Mines,* pp. 31–35, 73–75, 129–131.

88. S. Doc. 248, 59th Cong., 1st Sess. (Serial 4913), report dated February 27, 1906 [hereafter cited as *Taft Board Report*].

FIGURE 44. Endicott period installations for the protection of Boston Harbor included several batteries on Georges Island, the site of a Third System work named for Major General Joseph Warren, who was killed at the Battle of Bunker Hill, June 17, 1775. As space on the island for new construction was limited, some of the new works were superimposed on the crest of the existing structure. Nearest the camera in the photo are emplacements for one 10-inch and two 12-inch disappearing guns, sited along the east front of the 1833 work. Beyond and outside the early fort is a battery that mounted four 10-inch disappearing guns. To the right, just beyond the tree at the far end of the island, are three emplacements for 3-inch guns. (Photo by author and D. P. Kirchner, 1966)

FIGURE 45. During the Spanish-American War the remnant of Fort Sumter was largely filled in with earth, and a two-gun battery was built across the original structure. The new work was one of the very few constructed in which the guns, both 12-inch, were mounted on different types of carriages. Here, a barbette carriage is seen in the near emplacement, while the other contains a disappearing gun in the loading position. Named for Brigadier General Isaac Huger, Continental Army, this battery remained in service until about 1943. During World War II, the fort was also the site of a dual-purpose battery of 90-mm. guns installed for defense against both aircraft and motor torpedo boats. Fort Sumter became a national monument in 1948. (Photo 38-FCD-98, in the records of the Chief of Naval Operations, National Archives, about 1921)

FIGURE 46. Fort Washington, Maryland, located on the Potomac about ten miles below the national capital, displays three generations of harbor defense works within the space of a hundred yards. The masonry structure, though of general Third System style, was actually planned and begun prior to the convening of the Bernard Board to replace an earlier work that had been destroyed in 1814 to keep it from falling into British hands. Like three or four other forts begun late in the War of 1812 or shortly thereafter, Fort Washington cannot, strictly speaking, be categorized as belonging to either the Second or the Third System, but falls somewhere in between. Forward of the masonry work are the remnants of a V-shaped earthwork battery and a pair of Endicott period concrete emplacements built across the V, whose point is still faintly visible. The earthen battery, on one arm of which may be seen a 15-inch Rodman platform, was constructed during the early 1870s, on top of two earlier earthworks of roughly the same shape, the first dating from the 1820s or 1830s, the second from the Civil War. The Endicott period installation, for two 4-inch guns, was one of eight batteries constructed on the Fort Washington reservation between 1896 and 1905. (Photo 1058-I, National Park Service, 1965)

Figure 47. Typical of the manner in which Endicott period batteries were located with respect to older works was the siting of new installations on Staten Island, New York, around 1900. The pre-Civil War structures, Forts Richmond and Tompkins, are indicated, respectively, by the letters A and B on this photo, taken prior to the construction of the Verrazano-Narrows Bridge. Batteries constructed between 1896 and 1907 have been ringed. Those along the shore near Fort Richmond faced across the channel and had 3- and 4.7-inch rapid-fire guns, while the emplacements at the upper right, facing toward the ocean, were for 10- and 12-inch disappearing guns. Remnants of post-Civil War batteries are enclosed by broken rings. The concrete base of a World War I antiaircraft gun emplacement is circled at C, and the rectangle at D encloses the positions of four 3-inch guns moved here during World War II from their original emplacements just to the right of Fort Richmond. (Photo 674688, U.S. Navy, 1956)

as communications and powered ammunition handling), and, most important, a modern system of aiming for major-caliber guns and mortars.

The new aiming system represented the most significant advance to be made in harbor defense fire control until the introduction of radar in World War II. Prior to this time, aiming had generally been done from individual guns with the aid of elementary sighting instruments. Although a certain amount of progress had been made through the improvisation of new techniques, accuracy of fire against moving targets had remained largely a matter of art, experience, and educated guessing. The new system, in contrast, was based on a combination of optical instrumentation of great precision, the rapid processing of mathematical data, and the electrical transmission of target-sighting and gun-pointing information. Of the several methods of fire control devised at about this time, the most elaborate and precise made use, for a given battery, of two or more widely spaced sighting structures technically known as base-end stations. From these small buildings simultaneous optical bearings were continuously taken of a moving target, and the angles of sight were communicated repeatedly to a central battery computing room. Here the successive sightings were plotted and future target positions were predicted. Allowances were made and corrections worked in for meteorological factors and for such other variables as target progress during the projectile time of flight and during the time taken to calculate and transmit the various data. The computed products were then translated into aiming directions which were forwarded electrically to each gun emplacement or mortar pit.[89]

While such systems were beginning to be installed to permit the application of precise fire-control methods to harbor defense, basically similar techniques were, of course, under development for use in naval gunnery. For about the first decade of the twentieth century, however, the superiority of guns ashore over those on ships was probably greater than in any other period, largely because the distance between base-end stations along the coast was almost without practical limit, while the interval separating their counterparts afloat was necessarily restricted to a few yards. As a result, the advantage in accuracy of shore fire over naval gunnery increased rapidly with target distance, giving coastal armament a considerable margin of effectiveness beyond the point at which the precision of naval fire broke down. Thus, though there was no appreciable difference in terms of actual power between guns of the same caliber ashore and afloat, the former had a greater effective range until, toward the beginning of World War I, changes in the entire technique of shipboard fire direction began to reduce this advantage.[90]

89. Ibid., pp. 17–18, 36–39; Winslow, *Lectures*, pp. 118–147.
90. *Taft Board Report*, p. 18. The topic of naval gunnery during the early twentieth century is discussed in Arthur J. Marder, *From the Dreadnought to Scapa Flow: The*

With respect to major armament installations within the United States, where the Endicott period construction was already within a few percent of completion, the Taft Board's activities had comparatively limited relevance. Rather, its attention was directed chiefly to areas acquired as a result of the war with Spain, and in these places were to be seen the most visible effects of the Board's proposals. As had been done two decades earlier for continental harbors, defenses were now projected for ten positions in the new insular possessions and the Panama Canal Zone.[91]

The physical changes in the heavy gun installations commenced after 1906 were slight, for neither the carriages nor the battery structures of the Taft period differed materially from those of the Endicott period, except for their somewhat larger size, required to accommodate a new disappearing gun of 14-inch caliber. Partly because of this weapon's greater power and partly because of experience indicating that the armament density of the 1890s was unnecessarily high, spacing between batteries, though not particularly within, was increased; and the defenses constructed in the Philippines and Panama at this time included the first examples of single-gun installations at considerable distances from each other (see Figure 48).[92]

Only in the mortar installations was there a significant revision in battery design, brought about by the adoption of a new model mortar having a range and accuracy well beyond that of previous types. Because of this increase in weapon effectiveness, practically all of these batteries begun after about 1911, most of them outside the continental United States, were built for a reduced number of mortars—two per pit, four per battery.[93]

Finally, out of the program initiated by the Taft Board—though not envisioned by the Board itself—came a unique American defensive installation that merits special mention. This was Fort Drum (Figure 49), located in

---

Royal Navy in the Fisher Era, 1904–1919 (London: Oxford, 1961); Bernard Brodie, *Sea Power in the Machine Age* (Princeton: Princeton University Press, 1941); and Oscar Parkes, *British Battleships* (London: Seeley, 1957).

91. *Taft Board Report,* p. 12. The locations outside the continental limits were: Manila and Subic Bays in the Philippines; Guam; Pearl Harbor and Honolulu, Hawaii; Kiska Island in the Aleutians; Guantanamo, Cuba; San Juan, Puerto Rico; and the two entrances to the Panama Canal. Those actually fortified during this period are shown in Appendix A.

92. On Carabao and Caballo Islands, in the mouth of Manila Bay, the distances between the single-gun 14-inch batteries were, respectively, 1200 and 2000 feet.

93. Between the early 1890s and World War I, mortar installations underwent a systematic evolution characterized by a reduction, first, in the number of pits per battery and, later, in the number of mortars per pit. The original four-pit batteries (of four mortars per pit) were divided around 1906 into eight-mortar batteries of two pits each. A few years later the armament of most batteries was reduced again, from four to two mortars per pit. In existing installations half the weapons were actually removed, while new batteries were designed with two-mortar pits.

the mouth of Manila Bay on an island too small to be fortified with conventional emplacements. Employing a mode of construction used by several other nations but previously avoided by the United States because of cost, Army engineers turned for the first time to the use of armored turrets. A steel and concrete work was built in the form of a small ship, on the "deck" of which were mounted two pairs of 14-inch guns in turrets similar to those on battleships. With a cage mast to enhance the resemblance, the fort came to be known in the service as the "concrete battleship" and according to old Army folklore was sometimes mistaken at twilight for a moving ship by those aboard passing vessels.[94]

In the two decades between about 1890 and 1910—roughly the era here referred to as the Endicott and Taft periods—two noteworthy events took place which, though they did not affect fortification design or weaponry as such, were of direct relevance to harbor defense activity in the United States during the twentieth century. One was the assignment of artillery personnel to two new types of organizations within the Army; the other involved a change in the Navy's function with respect to coast defense.

Up to this time, the same regiments had performed both field and coast artillery service, but as weapons became more advanced they also became more specialized, and with the advent of modern rifled ordnance around 1890 the physical differences between field and seacoast armament were multiplied. Furthermore, while developments in field artillery were tactically oriented, i.e., toward increasing mobility and coordination with infantry and cavalry, the seacoast service was concerned largely with technical matters such as heavy ammunition handling, nighttime harbor illumination, and, especially, the sophisticated methods of fire control described above. As a result, a reorganization of the Army in 1901 created 30 batteries of field artillery and 126 companies of coast artillery. Each of the latter was roughly of a size appropriate to the manning of either a major-caliber gun or mortar battery, two or more rapid-fire batteries, or a mine battery. A few years later, in 1907, the number of seacoast units was increased to 170, and the two artillery components were formally established as distinct branches of the Army. These were to remain separate throughout both world wars and until 1950, when the Field Artillery and the Coast Artillery Corps, by that time composed exclusively of antiaircraft units, were reunited into a single Artillery branch.[95]

94. Louis Morton, *The Fall of the Philippines* (United States Army in World War II: The War in the Pacific; Washington: Department of the Army, 1953), pp. 476–478; James H. and William M. Belote, *Corregidor: The Saga of a Fortress* (New York: Harper & Row, 1967), p. 13.

95. 31 Stat. 748 (February 2, 1901); 34 Stat. 861 (January 25, 1907); 64 Stat. 263 (June 28, 1950).

FIGURE 48. A large, single-gun battery of the type constructed in the Philippines and the Panama Canal Zone as a result of the 1906 recommendations of the Taft Board. Consisting of a 14-inch disappearing gun, seen in the loading position, this battery was located near the west end of Caballo, one of the small fortified islands in the mouth of Manila Bay. A similar 14-inch gun was located two thousand feet eastward, beyond the high ridge. The island's defenses also included a pair of 6-inch guns, two 3-inch guns, and four 12-inch mortars (see Figure 65). (Photo, U.S. Navy, 1963)

FIGURE 49. Fort Drum, Manila Bay's "concrete battleship," was located on the island of El Fraile, which was cut to water level then surrounded by a concrete shell with an average thickness of about 27 feet. Some 350 feet in length, this structure was decked and compartmented to provide quarters, magazines, power generating rooms, fuel and water tanks, and storage rooms, all protected by many feet of reinforced concrete. The turrets for the four 14-inch guns, though of naval style, were designed by the Army and manufactured at Newport News, Virginia. Because weight was of less consequence here than in the building of ships, the armor and turning machinery of the turrets, as well as the ammunition handling equipment, were considerably heavier than corresponding armament components designed for use afloat. The fort's secondary armament consisted of a pair of 6-inch guns (one above the other in an armored casemate), on each side of the structure. Built between 1909 and 1919, and named for Brigadier General Richard C. Drum, a veteran of the Mexican and Civil Wars, this work was a nearly impregnable self-contained stronghold. Of all the Manila Bay fortifications, it alone remained effective until the moment of Corregidor's surrender to the Japanese on May 6, 1942. (Photos by Colonel George Ruhlen, 1938)

The period around the turn of the century also marked a fundamental change in the relationship between the harbor defenses and the Navy, for these were the years during which the fleet was transformed from a force devoted largely to immediate continental protection into an instrument of genuine sea power. Throughout most of our earlier history, the Navy had been constrained to a variety of limited positive roles such as worldwide squadron cruising to protect American commerce, and, in theory, commerce raiding. At the same time, many Administrations and the majority of Congresses had been concerned chiefly with the Navy's defensive mission. As a result, a great deal of attention for nearly a hundred years was directed toward maintaining a fleet for defensive purposes and toward equipping it in keeping with the coast defense orientation that represented a conceptual outgrowth of the Jeffersonian gunboat policy.[96]

Throughout the nineteenth century precisely what constituted the Navy's coast defense function varied with changes in materiel and tactics; at any given moment, its exact nature was imperfectly agreed upon not only by Congressmen and the public but by military and naval professionals as well. Some saw this role of the fleet as a simple extension of the harbor defenses; others saw it as a means of covering the long, unfortified stretches of coast; still others, as a complete and possibly more economical substitute for fortifications. But whatever the view, there was agreement that the Navy was to perform the same general function as the fortifications, either as a parallel or an adjunctive agency, or as an alternative to them. This unmistakable emphasis on the Navy's passive defense role was reflected in a succession of ponderous, heavily gunned, but often unseaworthy developments, many of them experimental only, which included Fulton's *Demologous* of 1814, the various pre-1860 "steam batteries," the monitors, retained long after the Civil War, the floating batteries proposed by the Endicott Board, and the so-called "sea-going coastal [or coast-line] battleships" of the 1890s.[97]

Certain officers had long understood and urged, to no avail, that the Navy should not be tied down and dispersed in defense of coasts or harbors, but rather given freedom to exercise as a concentrated force its appropriate function: to capture and destroy the enemy's fleet in distant waters, to intercept his commerce, to blockade his ports, and, in short, to command the high seas. Among Army engineers of the pre-Civil War era, for example, both Totten and Halleck had recognized this positive fleet principle, which Great Britain had in fact been following for more than two centuries, and both also appear to have considered a major function of seacoast forts to

96. For discussions of the defensive emphasis in nineteenth-century American naval policy, see Millis, *Arms and Men,* and Harold and Margaret Sprout, *The Rise of American Naval Power, 1776–1918* (Princeton: Princeton University Press, 1939).

97. Sprout, *Naval Power,* p. 213; Millis, *Arms and Men,* p. 158; *Taft Board Report,* pp. 41–42.

be that of contributing to the Navy's offensive role by providing security for its bases and repair facilities.[98] Not, however, until the 1890s, after it had been articulated publicly for the first time by Alfred Thayer Mahan, did this command-of-the-seas concept begin to gain widespread circulation and acceptance. During the twelve or fifteen years that followed, the general reconstruction of the fleet already in progress, the Spanish-American War and this country's entry onto the world stage, and the decided Mahanistic navalism of Theodore Roosevelt all contributed heavily to a fundamental transformation of the Navy and to the elimination for all time of the passive coast-defense doctrine as a basic element of American naval policy.

Addressing a conference at the Naval War College early in 1908, Roosevelt left no doubt as to either the completeness of the transformation itself or, in line with it, the role to be taken by the harbor defenses in assisting the Navy's positive function:

Let the port be protected by the [Army's] fortifications; the fleet must be foot-loose to search out and destroy the enemy's fleet; that is the function of the fleet; that is the only function that can justify the fleet's existence . . . For the protection of our coasts we need fortifications; not merely to protect the salient points of our possessions, but we need them so that the Navy can be foot-loose.[99]

The Navy's interests were served in several ways by the existence of powerful fortifications. Not the least of these, particularly in post-Spanish-American-War thinking, was the sense of security provided by the presence of strong defenses near the major cities, which could do much to avert the kind of panic that had led early in the war to a public outcry for coastal protection along the Atlantic seaboard and consequently threatened to fragment the fleet for this purpose.[100] But the chief reason for such defenses, from the Navy's point of view, was the protection of its operating and repair bases. This requirement came to be an increasingly important factor in the location of new fortifications throughout the period beginning with the Taft Board, whose project had been the first to include a large proportion of harbors which, having neither commercial significance nor neighbor-

98. Totten, *National Defences,* p. 18; Halleck, *Elements,* pp. 194–197, 202; Sprout, *Naval Power,* p. 205. See also *Taft Board Report* (pp. 21–22), which suggests that the members of both this Board and the Endicott Board recognized that "the legitimate field of action of a regular naval force is upon the high seas in meeting and destroying the enemy's fleet."

99. Quoted by Major William G. Haan in a lecture at the Coast Artillery School, Fort Monroe, July 1908. The conference is referred to by Sprout (*Naval Power,* p. 279).

100. Sprout, *Naval Power,* pp. 234ff. Mahan's concern with fortifications for this reason is suggested on page 236. The episode continued to be recalled as late as 1941, when it was brought up in House hearings to justify large harbor defense expenditures (U.S., Congress, House, Committee on Appropriations, *Military Establishment Appropriation Bill for 1942, Hearings,* before a subcommittee of the Committee on Appropriations, House of Representatives, 77th Cong., 1st Sess., 1941, p. 574).

ing cities, were solely of naval significance.[101] During the ensuing years, although the construction and operation of the harbor defenses continued to be responsibilities of the Army, decisions relating to their preservation or abandonment depended more and more on their dispensability so far as the Navy was concerned, and by World War II the fleet's needs in this connection had become the principal, if not the sole reason for the retention of existing fortifications and the installation of new ones. World War II was also the first occasion during the twentieth century on which the Navy itself participated to any extent in the specific mechanics of harbor defense, when it planted contact mines to supplement the Army's electrically controlled minefields, installed and operated various types of net and boom defenses, and conducted destroyer patrols beyond harbor entrances.[102]

World War I and the Post-War Years

The extravagant proposals put forth by the Endicott Board in 1886 were never fully realized, nor was the less ambitious project recommended by the Taft Board twenty years later, but the efforts of these two groups nevertheless led to an overlapping two-stage fortification program of a magnitude which, for the second time, gave the United States a system of harbor defenses unexcelled by those of any other nation.

Even before the last of the Taft period installations were commenced, however, developments within certain of the world's navies were beginning to present a serious technical challenge to all existing harbor defenses, foreign as well as American. The dozen years following the Russo-Japanese War were highly productive to the advancement of naval guns and gunnery. Significant improvements in fire-control techniques, initiated mainly by Great Britain, enabled battleships to engage enemy vessels at distances that formerly would have exceeded their limits of accurate shooting (though not the actual reach of their guns). In other words, the usable ranges of naval guns now approached the maximum ranges of which these guns were already capable.[103] In addition, the introduction, around the beginning of World War I, of battleship turrets of new designs began a trend toward higher firing angles, which led to extended maximum ranges, and equally impor-

101. *Taft Board Report,* p. 4.

102. Conn, *Guarding the United States,* pp. 46, 50–51. For a statement regarding the Navy's insistence on the modernization of the harbor defenses in the World War II period, see *Military Establishment Appropriation Bill for 1942, Hearings,* p. 572.

103. Marder, *Dreadnought to Scapa Flow,* pp. 414–416; Brodie, *Sea Power in the Machine Age,* pp. 230–232; Donald Macintyre, *The Thunder of The Guns* (New York: Norton, 1959), pp. 165–167.

tant, altered the character of naval gunfire by producing greater curvatures of projectile trajectories. Shells could thus be directed not only against the armored sides of ships, as before, when gunnery had been restricted to flat-trajectory fire, but also onto relatively unprotected horizontal surfaces such as decks.

The implication of these developments with respect to the fortifications of the United States was devastating. By 1916 several foreign battleships could already outrange by a substantial margin any harbor defense weapon within this country's continental limits. Moreover, the plunging type of fire which these vessels could now deliver nullified the principal protective advantages inherent in the disappearing carriage on which seven of every eight heavy American seacoast guns were mounted.

In response to this significant progress afloat, ordnance specialists turned to designing an entire new generation of coastal armament. In the meantime, however, the United States entered the war and became occupied with matters far more urgent than a major modernization of its coastal defenses. Fortunately this conflict did not seriously threaten American shores, and wartime installation activities were therefore limited. A few permanent batteries were commenced for the new armament, and a number of older pieces (mostly 5- and 6-inch guns) were shifted from their home emplacements to rapidly erected works in previously undefended positions, most of which were abandoned within a year or two of the armistice.

The personnel of the Coast Artillery Corps, however, were not idle during the war, and a great many went overseas with new types of units, for beyond its traditional assignment to the fixed armament of the harbor defenses, the Corps was made responsible for the operation of certain new types of artillery materiel, two of which were to remain permanently under its jurisdiction. As a result, a division in terms of troop organization, functions, tactics, and operating techniques was made according to three basic classes of armament: fixed harbor defense weapons, mobile seacoast artillery, and antiaircraft guns. This three-way split was to persist for some thirty years beyond World War I.

The antiaircraft function had originally been assigned to the Coast Artillery because of its background in firing against moving targets and its experience with the kind of rapid data handling involved in such firing. After the war, considerable attention began to be given to the development of both fixed and mobile antiaircraft armament, as well as of various accessory equipment such as searchlights, aircraft sound locators, and mechanical fire-direction calculators.[104]

104. By the mid-1920s, the space being devoted by the professional journals such as the *Coast Artillery Journal* to the subjects of antiaircraft techniques and materiel was approaching that given to the traditional seacoast defense topics.

Contrary to most contemporary impressions regarding Army thinking of the 1920s, this period witnessed a rapid, widespread, and somewhat prophetic turning of interest within the Coast Artillery toward antiaircraft defense, which was ultimately to constitute the Corps' sole function. In this and the following decade, many fixed antiaircraft weapons were emplaced, usually in three-gun batteries, to furnish protection for permanent seacoast works. Most of the pieces were wartime 3-inch models, but a few, all mounted in the Canal Zone, were of a later 105-millimeter type.

Such installations continued until about the beginning of World War II, when the antiaircraft function was given over almost entirely to mobile 3-inch and, later, 90-millimeter armament, which was produced in large numbers throughout the war. This aspect of the Coast Artillery's duties grew tremendously between 1940 and 1945, and antiaircraft became in effect though not in name a new part of the Army, separate from and much larger than its parent branch. When, a few years later, the Corps was finally abolished, antiaircraft artillery was its sole component.

The mobile coastal armament of the post-World War I period had not originally been designed for seacoast use, but came instead from a large stock of long-range weapons on hand at the time of the armistice. Practically all these had been produced for employment on the mainland of Europe, and many had, in fact, already been manned during the war by Coast Artillery personnel.[105] The availability of this materiel, together with a postwar doctrine that placed great emphasis on mobility, prompted an entirely different approach to harbor defense which, throughout the period between the two world wars, was to parallel the traditional mainstream represented by the fixed armament and the permanent fortifications.

Mobile seacoast artillery was of two general types, railway and tractor-drawn. The heaviest items remained from a wartime program under which several hundred existing weapons of between 7- and 14-inch caliber—some supplied by the Navy, and some "borrowed" from Endicott period batteries—were to have been mounted on railway carriages produced by various manufacturers of heavy equipment such as locomotives and steam shovels. Because of the extensive planning, designing, and retooling involved, however, the carriage production had progressed slowly, and by the time the war

105. For accounts of World War I production of long-range mobile artillery, see Benedict Crowell, *America's Munitions* (Washington: GPO, 1919), pp. 56–102; Benedict Crowell and Robert Forrest Wilson, *The Armies of Industry* (New Haven: Yale University Press, 1921), vol. 1, pp. 63–128. For troop dispositions and assignments, see Army War College, *Order of Battle of the United States Land Forces in the World War (1917–1919); American Expeditionary Forces; General Headquarters, Armies, Army Corps, Services of Supply, and Separate Forces* (Washington: GPO, 1937), pp. 82, 83, 151–152.

ended barely a dozen railway units had actually been shipped overseas, although approximately two hundred were finally manufactured.[106] The materiel taken from among this large stock of railway pieces for postwar seacoast service comprised three models: an 8-inch gun, a 12-inch mortar, and a 14-inch gun. The first two came directly from the existing stock; the third was a 1920 improvement of a wartime experimental piece.

Also left over from the war were a great many weapons of various medium-caliber models which did not require rail transport but could be moved by road. Among the most powerful of these was a 155-millimeter gun—an Americanized version of a 1917 French design—of which several hundred were on hand. This became the standard tractor-drawn weapon for seacoast use against secondary targets and, with carriage modifications and the addition of pneumatic tires, it remained in service throughout most of World War II.[107]

From a technical standpoint, both railway and tractor-drawn weapons had serious limitations as harbor defense armament. Among the most important was their lack of accuracy compared to that of fixed guns, which had the benefit of solid, steady firing platforms, and which were tied in with great precision to permanent, precalibrated fire-control networks. An equally serious shortcoming lay in the carriage designs, which allowed neither the 155s nor the heavier railway pieces to swivel horizontally with the rapidity or to the extent required for use against moving targets. To some degree, these problems were met by the construction of rather simple circular concrete bases at potential firing points. But though such prepared positions improved steadiness and provided adequate lateral sweep, their use effectively tied the weapons to semi-fixed emplacements which still lacked most of the advantages inherent in permanent installations.[108]

Only in a few highly unusual situations, mainly outside the continental United States, was the employment of mobile seacoast artillery peculiarly favored by circumstances of geography. Because of the limited size of the Island of Oahu, for example, railway and tractor-drawn pieces were not only useful in a harbor defense role at Honolulu and Pearl Harbor, but could cover most of the land perimeter and thus function in an overall coast defense role as well. Again, a pair of 14-inch railway guns maintained in the Canal Zone constituted a unique reserve that could be shifted from one

106. U.S., Congress, House, Select Committee on Expenditures in the War Department, *Hearings,* before Subcommittee No. 5 (Ordnance) of the Select Committee, House of Representatives, 66th Cong., 1st Sess., Serial 6, vol. 1, Exhibit 3.

107. War Department Technical Manual, TM 4–210 (Seacoast Artillery Weapons), 15 October 1944, pp. 135ff.

108. Manuscript draft history of the design, development, and production of railway artillery, prepared approximately August 1945, in the Artillery Division, Industrial Services, Ordnance Department, Army Service Forces (in RG 156, NA). See also Conn, *Guarding the United States,* pp. 49–50, on the vulnerability of railway artillery.

FIGURE 50. During World War I more than three hundred seacoast guns and mortars of 5- to 12-inch caliber were taken from their permanent batteries for use as mobile artillery weapons. Whereas the lighter pieces were equipped with carriages that could be moved along roads by horses or tractors, the larger caliber weapons were mounted on newly designed railway carriages. Included among the latter were nearly fifty 8-inch guns of the type shown here, but by the time the war ended in November 1918, only three of these had been sent overseas. After the armistice some of the smaller guns were returned to their original emplacements at the forts and others were declared obsolete and scrapped, but most of the railway guns were retained as mobile units for future use in coast defense. During the 1920s and 1930s the majority of these were stored, though some 8-inch guns remained in the hands of Coast Artillery troops, mainly at Fort Hancock, New Jersey, and at the Chesapeake Bay entrance. About a dozen others were shipped to Hawaii in 1934, where the two shown here were photographed at Fort Kamehameha around 1937. During World War II similar units were sent to the new bases which had been acquired from Great Britain in exchange for old American destroyers. A few guns of this model were also turned over to Canada for use in British Columbia. (Photo, courtesy Master Sergeant Edwin Bartcher, about 1937)

FIGURE 51. Most numerous among the railway artillery weapons produced by this country for World War I were the 12-inch mortars, nearly a hundred of which were assembled from newly manufactured carriages and cradles and existing mortars drawn from Endicott period batteries (see Figure 40). This 1918 photo, taken at Aberdeen Proving Ground, Maryland, shows the first completed unit, equipped with European type railway couplings, and painted in the somewhat bizarre style of camouflage popular at the time. The railway car and basic carriage was similar to that of the 8-inch gun shown in Figure 50, but the mortar itself was almost entirely enclosed within a cast steel cradle that held the various elements of the recoil and elevating mechanisms. Most of these mobile mortars were stored between the two World Wars, first at Fort Eustis, Virginia, and after about 1930 at Aberdeen. Eight were sent to Hawaii in 1921, however, and a dozen more were kept in service at Fort Hancock, around the Chesapeake Bay area, and in the Pacific Northwest until early 1942 when, along with the stored units, they were scrapped. (Photo 111-SC-25735, U.S. Army Signal Corps, in the National Archives, 1918)

FIGURE 52. The 14-inch Model 1920 was the largest American railway gun and the first produced expressly for seacoast defense. The 8- and 12-inch mobile weapons had been designed primarily in response to a wartime requirement for heavy battlefield artillery, and their postwar adoption for seacoast service was largely a matter of expediency. There had also been four separate 14-inch railway gun designs during the war, two of which were still in the blueprint stage when hostilities ended. The other two were developed independently by the Navy's Bureau of Ordnance, and about a dozen carriages for existing Navy guns were manufactured in record time by the Baldwin Locomotive Works. Five of these reached Europe in mid-1918 and, manned by naval personnel under the command of Rear Admiral Charles P. Plunkett, were the largest American artillery weapons to serve in France. None of the four 14-inch designs, however, was suitable for use against moving targets, so the Army's Ordnance Department turned to still another model, which had been under development and test since 1916, and reworked it completely to incorporate the best features of both the Army and Navy wartime designs, including the gun tube of the Navy model. The result was the dual-purpose Model 1920. This weapon could be prepared for fire against stationary land targets in a matter of hours. It was necessary only to bolster the carriage with steel I-beams laid between the tracks and to extend and dig in a set of outriggers. In this type of emplacement (above), the gun could be traversed through about seven degrees, which was normally sufficient for aiming corrections once it had been set up on a stretch of track pointed generally toward the target. For seacoast use, the weapon was brought by rail to a prepared emplacement, positioned directly over a circular concrete foundation block, and lowered onto it. The railway trucks were then withdrawn, and the carriage could be traversed through a full 360 degrees. Shown below is one of several such emplacements in the Panama Canal Zone, where two guns of this model were maintained, capable of being moved from one ocean to the other in a day or less. A pair of similar guns was based at San Pedro, California. Though some consideration was given to using them in Europe during the latter part of World War II, they remained in the Los Angeles area throughout the war and for a year or two beyond. (Photos, top, 19489, U.S. Army Ordnance Department, 1924; bottom, in author's collection, 1929)

FIGURE 53. During World War I the French 155-mm. gun, a heavy tractor-drawn weapon, was put into production with slight modifications by the United States as the Model 1918. Known more commonly in the American service as the GPF (Grande Puissance Filloux), this gun was the most widely used of the mobile artillery pieces adopted for seacoast defense after the war. Although the carriage of the 155 allowed a wider scope of traverse than the average for guns designed for field use, the lateral movement was still insufficient for fire against moving targets. During the 1920s, however, a simple and relatively inexpensive platform was devised, consisting essentially of a segment of curved rail embedded in concrete, along which the gun's twin trails could easily be moved. This type of emplacement (left) was initially developed and tested in the Canal Zone and thus came to be known as the Panama mount. The GPF was greatly improved between the two world wars, mainly to increase its mobility by providing it with modern wheels and pneumatic tires in place of the old cast-steel wheels. It was used throughout the 1920s and 1930s to train thousands of reserve and National Guard coast artillerymen, and after Pearl Harbor was rushed in large numbers to guard unfortified positions along both coasts. It subsequently proved to be particularly useful in the war zones and served as the principal coast defense weapon on a number of Pacific islands. Late in the war, however, the GPF began to be replaced by the new 155 (right), which had been developed in the United States between the wars, and which had a range about fifty percent greater than that of the Model 1918. Designed as a heavy field artillery piece and popularly known during World War II and since as the "Long Tom," the new weapon was brought into seacoast service with a circular steel platform that could be transported easily and assembled rapidly. The new 155 is shown here at Angaur Island, in the western Carolines, in April 1945. An additional emplacement may be seen being assembled in the background. (Photos, U.S. Army Signal Corps: A, about 1929; B, SC-248874, 1945)

FIGURE 54. The last mobile weapon developed in this country for
seacoast service consisted of a Navy-designed 8-inch gun on an Army-
designed railway carriage. A large number of such guns, rendered
surplus in the early 1920s as a result of the Washington Naval Treaty,
were made available to the Army. On hand at the time was a single
experimental 12-inch railway howitzer which had been manufactured
during the war but never put into production. With some modification
its carriage was adapted to take the Navy gun, and the pilot model
thus assembled, almost entirely from existing components, was completed at relatively low cost. It is shown in the photo above, taken
at Aberdeen Proving Ground in 1938. After war broke out in Europe,
this weapon was put into production, and by the time of Pearl Harbor
practically the entire order of some two dozen units was completed.
During the war two of the guns were assigned to the defenses of Puget
Sound, and two more to Los Angeles. The remainder were left on the
east coast, mainly at Fort Hancock, New Jersey, at Fort Miles at the
mouth of the Delaware River, and at Fort John Custis at the entrance
to Chesapeake Bay. (Photo, U.S. Army Ordnance Department, 1938)

ocean to the other within a few hours and positioned on prepared foundations.

These instances, however, were atypical in that they involved small areas. In general the rapid movement of railway weapons over long distances was not feasible, and their mobility was therefore only strategic, not tactical. In other words, such armament might be sent to a given location for an extended period, either to augment existing defenses or to provide protection during the construction of permanent works. But there was no validity to the notion, attractive as it might have been to economy-minded laymen and members of appropriations subcommittees, that railway artillery could, or was intended to eliminate the need for costly fixed installations. This idea, voiced on occasion by individual enthusiasts within the Army, did not reflect the official War Department position, which maintained the continuing necessity of permanent batteries for defense against capital ships. To envision future naval threats being met by mobile weapons that could be dispatched from a central pool in an emergency to rush to this harbor or that over commercial railway lines was simply to ignore the genuine limitations of the equipment.[109]

The reasons for employing mobile seacoast artillery at all were, of course, primarily economic—the guns were available at a time, after World War I, when the immediate future held little hope for large military appropriations of any sort. Because the 1920s and 1930s in fact produced only a very few modern fixed batteries, mobile artillery continued to be used, chiefly at vital locations for which new permanent works had been authorized but not yet funded. Once large sums again became available for the construction of fixed harbor defense installations, after the outbreak of World War II, all mobile coast artillery was relegated to secondary roles, either to provide interim protection pending the completion of new permanent works, or to defend less vital positions which had no fixed armament. Most of the older railway equipment was scrapped as new batteries were completed, though a few items went to Allied nations.[110]

In contrast both with the fortifications of previous eras and with the mobile artillery of the same period, the post-World War I generation of permanent works was neither extensive nor complex. It did, however, introduce the largest and most powerful item of service artillery ever produced by the United States.

109. On the useful mobility of railway artillery, see, for example, U.S., Congress, House, Committee on Appropriations, *Military Establishment Appropriation Bill for 1939, Hearings,* before a subcommitte of the Committee on Appropriations, House of Representatives, 75th Cong., 3d Sess., 1938, pp. 416–417.

110. Conn, *Guarding the United States,* pp. 49–50; miscellaneous inventories of seacoast artillery materiel, in RG 156, NA.

This body of fixed defenses had its beginnings around 1915, as indicated earlier, when marked advances in naval gunnery made it necessary to increase the range of coastal armament considerably. Two principal weapons were developed to meet this requirement. The first, produced in time to be installed in a small number of batteries commenced during the war, was essentially an emergency expedient. It consisted of a newly designed high-angle barbette carriage (Figure 55) that nearly doubled the range of an existing model Endicott period 12-inch gun. The construction of batteries based on this combination continued after the war, the last of them being completed in the early 1920s, at just about the time the second type of armament became available for installation. This was a completely new 16-inch gun (Figure 56) that had an extreme range of nearly thirty miles with a projectile weighing more than a ton. At the time, it was the most powerful cannon in the world, and it remained capable of outshooting practically any battleship ever built, probably even the gigantic Japanese *Yamato* class vessels of World War II with their 18.1-inch guns.[111]

While the first few of these 16-inch pieces were still being installed, a number of new and only slightly less powerful naval weapons of the same caliber unexpectedly became available to the Army as a result of the 1922 Washington Naval Treaty (under the terms of which construction of several capital ships was canceled, leaving the Navy with no foreseeable use for the guns already produced for them). Since the Army guns were extremely expensive and time consuming to manufacture, the few additional 16-inch batteries constructed during the 1920s and 1930s, as well as the many more built during World War II, were all armed with these naval weapons on Army-designed carriages (Figure 57).[112]

Although this postwar armament represented a tremendous advance over that in existence as of 1915, the new fortification works were themselves characterized by remarkable design simplicity. Security of the defenses against naval fire lay almost entirely in the wide separation of their various elements, and the weapons were provided with no material protection of any sort. To some extent, they were concealed, but only from sea-level observation. From above, the emplacements were almost literal bull's-eyes of concrete, designed to allow the guns at their centers to turn a full 360 degrees.

The principle of protective dispersion which at this time governed harbor defense design led to the construction of the most extended of all American seacoast fortification works. Endicott and even Taft period installations had

111. War Department Field Manual, FM 4–155 (Coast Artillery Field Manual: Reference Data), 1 October 1940, pp. 7–8; Office of the Chief of Ordnance, *American Coast Artillery Materiel* (Washington: GPO, 1923).

112. Miscellaneous letters in [Navy] BuOrd Files 40163/69, /172, and /656; D. P. Kirchner and E. R. Lewis, "American Harbor Defenses: The Final Era," *United States Naval Institute Proceedings,* vol. 94, no. 1 (January 1968), 88–89, 95.

FIGURE 55. Long-range 12-inch gun on barbette carriage, Model 1917. The 10- and 12-inch guns installed during the Endicott period originally had a range of less than eight miles. Though extended a mile or two as a result of certain carriage modifications made after 1915, this range did not begin to approach the increase required to meet the strides being made in naval gunnery around the beginning of World War I. Because wartime efforts were directed toward the development and manufacture of weapons for use overseas, production of a completely new seacoast gun was out of the question; instead, a relatively simple new carriage was designed to make use of a stock of 12-inch guns maintained as spares for Endicott batteries. The new carriage, which afforded a firing elevation better than twice that of the disappearing and old barbette designs, increased the range to more than 17 miles. About a dozen batteries, each armed with a pair of these new weapons, were constructed between 1917 and 1923 and remained in service through World War II. The photo above was taken during a 1940 target practice by Battery Wallace, near San Francisco, named for Colonel Elmer J. Wallace, a Coast Artillery officer killed in France in 1918. (Photo, in author's collection, by T. J. McDonough, 1940)

FIGURE 56. Although heavier experimental cannon have been manufactured in this country, the largest and most powerful ever to be
produced as a standard piece was the 16-inch gun, Model 1919. The
barrel alone weighed nearly 200 tons and cost over $300,000. The
carriage weighed more than a million pounds, and, though relatively
simple in design, demanded components of a high degree of precision.
Manufacture required up to three years per unit. Very few of these
weapons were completed before a more economical and only slightly
less powerful substitute (see Figure 57) became available. The gun
shown above was one of a pair of Model 1919s installed between
1921 and 1924 at the west side of the entrance to Pearl Harbor. With
a range of nearly 50,000 yards, these weapons had a field of fire that
completely encircled the Island of Oahu and reached beyond its
shores at every point. (Photo 111-SC-100948, U.S. Army Signal Corps,
in the National Archives, 1927)

FIGURE 57. Under the terms of the Washington Naval Treaty of 1922, the United States suspended the construction of two new classes of capital ships comprising a total of 12 vessels, which were to have been armed with a new model 16-inch gun. At the time of the cancellation, most of this armament had already been manufactured, and a number of the guns were shortly thereafter transferred to the Army. Though lighter and less powerful than the Army guns of the same caliber, these weapons were immediately adopted for seacoast service and fitted to a modified version of the Model 1919 carriage. No additional guns of the Army model were produced, and from about 1925 on the naval weapon was used in all 16-inch installations. Shown above is one of the two guns of Battery Murray, the first work to be armed with the Navy weapon. Constructed near the Pacific end of the Panama Canal between 1925 and 1929, and named for Major General Arthur Murray, the Army's first Chief of Coast Artillery (1908 to 1911), this battery was laid out along typical post-World War I lines, with the guns spaced nearly a thousand feet apart for protection by dispersion. The emplacements were designed to permit 360-degree fields of fire but were neither concealed nor protected from above. During World War II most such batteries, both 16- and 12-inch, were reconstructed to provide their guns with substantial overhead cover. (Photo 111-SC-98611R, U.S. Army Signal Corps, in the National Archives, taken by Army Air Corps, 1932)

been relatively compact by comparison, with weapons of the same battery rarely more than two hundred feet apart. Now, however, 16-inch guns within the same battery were separated by as much as one thousand feet and linked, in some instances, by small railways which provided ammunition service from several distant and widely dispersed magazines.[113] Most of the 12-inch installations were considerably less spread out than this. Ammunition was stored in underground concrete magazines located between the emplacements, which were generally four to five hundred feet apart.

Of this brief post-World War I generation of defenses, which comprised a modest total of fewer than two dozen batteries, almost nothing remains. With only a few exceptions, every installation was subsequently absorbed into the final, World War II program of construction and modified accordingly, much as the works of the pre-1812 program had been assimilated over a century earlier into the Third System.

The Era of World War II

By the mid-1930s, the increasing threat posed to permanent harbor defense artillery by long-range and carrier-borne aircraft could no longer be disregarded. A certain number of additional fixed antiaircraft installations were projected (some to be completed as late as 1940), but these could not be counted upon for absolute protection of targets as crucial as heavy coastal batteries, for whose destruction an attacking seaborne force might well be willing to accept sizable aircraft losses.

An entirely new type of battery was therefore designed in which all components—armament, magazines, and various accessory equipment—were to be provided with substantial overhead cover, and construction of the prototype began at San Francisco in 1937. This installation (Figure 58) consisted of a pair of 16-inch guns within enormous casemates six hundred feet apart, between which extended a series of galleries housing the ammunition magazines, electrical power generators, and certain of the storage and operating facilities. The entire battery structure, designed to withstand direct hits from battleship projectiles or aerial bombs of equivalent energy, was roofed along its full length by eight to ten feet of densely reinforced concrete and up to twenty additional feet of earth. Directly over the casemates, from which only the gun barrels protruded through heavy armor shields, the concrete cover was even more massive.[114]

113. See, for example, battery construction plans, Drawer 155, Sheets 106–69 and 106–70, RG 77, NA, Cartographic Branch.
114. Reports of Completed Works, Harbor Defenses of San Francisco (Battery Richmond P. Davis), RG 77, NA.

During the next three years a few similar batteries were projected and begun in order to augment existing armament at particularly critical localities. But by 1940, the rapidly growing emphasis on national defense in general demanded, among other things, a greatly accelerated and expanded battery installation schedule. A special War Department board was convened to draft for the continental United States a new master harbor defense plan, and subsequently this was combined with several individual projects prepared for various positions outside the continental limits. The result, an extremely comprehensive program of construction, was ultimately to produce a system of seacoast fortifications that covered 33 locations throughout an area bounded by Dutch Harbor, Hawaii, the Canal Zone, Trinidad, Bermuda, and Newfoundland.[115]

In terms of battery types, the World War II fortifications were among the least varied ever constructed by this country, for both weapons and installation designs were standardized to an unprecedented degree. With a few exceptions, the entire spectrum of artillery requirements for harbor defense was covered by only two classes of armament, the primary-caliber 16-inch (naval) gun of the 1920s, and a newly developed 6-inch secondary piece with a 15-mile range. Practically all the dozen or so World War I high-angle 12-inch batteries were retained as well, and a new carriage was designed for use with a very small number of surplus 8-inch naval guns which had been in storage since the 1920s.[116]

These four modern weapons superseded more than two dozen separate models of six different calibers remaining as of 1940 from the Endicott and Taft periods, and their adoption for the World War II program thus effected great savings. Not only did their tremendous ranges significantly extend the defensive coverage over harbor approaches and thereby reduce the numbers of batteries and personnel required; but the fact that so few models were involved meant considerable simplifications in tactics, training, maintenance, ammunition manufacture and handling, and other aspects of supply. As a side benefit of this sweeping replacement of pre-World War I armament, a number of the older weapons still of value became available

115. Conn, *Guarding the United States,* pp. 46–47; Kirchner, "The Final Era," p. 98; Memo, Logistics Group for ACofS, OPD, 24 October 1945, Subj: Modernization Program for Seacoast Defenses (OPD 660.2 [24 Oct 45]); Memo, Chief of Coast Artillery for WPD, 4 October 1941, Subj: Priorities for Seacoast Batteries (AG 660.2 [10–4–41]). Jamaica was also included in the original project but was subsequently dropped; see Appendix A.

116. War Department TM 4–210, pp. 74–77, 89, 104–107, 113–115. Several dozen 3-inch guns of Endicott vintage were also retained for use against small fast vessels such as motor torpedo boats. These began to be replaced in 1943 by a newly designed 90-millimeter gun on a fixed mount which could be used against either surface or air craft. See TM 4–210, pp. 123–124, 129ff.; also, Conn, *Guarding the United States,* pp. 50–51.

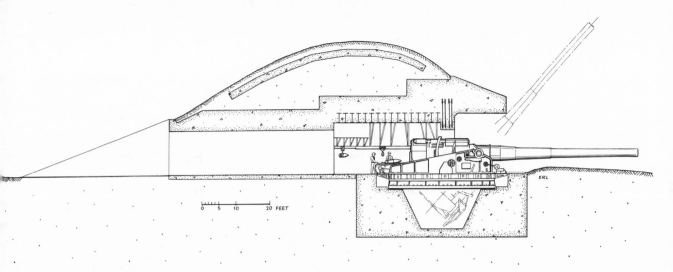

FIGURE 58. Battery Richmond P. Davis was constructed at San Francisco between 1937 and 1940. Named for a distinguished Coast Artillery Corps officer who died not long after it was commenced, this work was the model for all subsequent heavy-caliber seacoast batteries built by the United States. The two 16-inch Navy guns were protected by 13-foot reinforced concrete ceilings and several feet of earth. Essential battery components such as power generators and magazines were similarly protected, and the one-ton shells were transported to the guns by overhead trolleys on rails suspended from the ceilings. The cross section of the right casemate, above, shows some of the structural features and the magnitude and distribution of the protective members. The two-foot concrete layer just below the surface of the earth cover was known as a "burster course," and was designed to detonate bombs or projectiles before they penetrated to the principal structure. It was eliminated from the designs of most later batteries, whose ceilings were increased considerably in thickness. Though Battery Davis was never precisely duplicated, its essential form was used as the basis for all new 16-inch gun installations as well as for the modernization of most of the 16- and 12-inch batteries of the 1920s and 1930s. (Drawing by author)

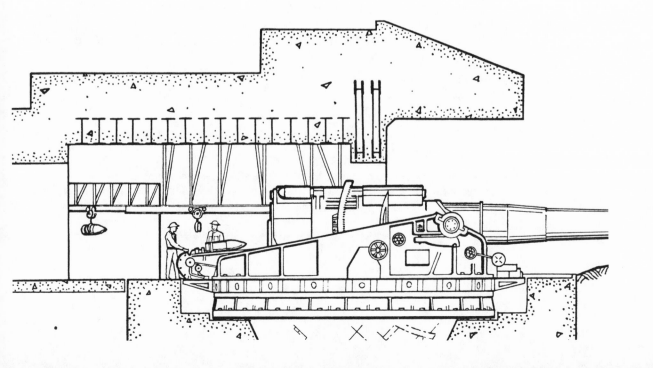

for release to Allied nations, which re-emplaced them to guard their own harbors.[117]

With regard to the new fortification structures, the installations constructed under this program followed, virtually without exception, a design uniformity found in no previous period. Aside from minor variations imposed by local factors such as topography and soil conditions, all batteries of the same armament caliber were essentially identical. Moreover, there was no appreciable dissimilarity between those of different calibers except with respect to size and to the nature of the overhead protection provided for the armament. All batteries, regardless of caliber, had two guns.

Sixteen- and 12-inch guns, whether newly installed or retained from the interwar period, were emplaced within reinforced concrete casemates (or "bunkers," as they are popularly called today). In most instances a heavy armor shield surrounded the forward part of the carriage and reduced the front opening of the casemate (Figure 59). Although such emplacements restricted the horizontal field of fire to less than 180 degrees, this limitation was rarely critical and was regarded as wholly justified in view of the protection afforded.

The new 6-inch guns were not casemated, but were provided instead with all around curved shields of cast steel four to six inches thick (see Figure 60), which furnished protection against machine-gun and light cannon fire, and all except direct hits by heavier projectiles or bombs. Of the very few new 8-inch batteries, one was casemated; the others were to have been fitted with a larger version of the 6-inch-type shield, but these shields never went into production.

The remaining portions of all batteries basically followed the 16-inch prototype. The earth-covered concrete structure located between the two guns housed most of the ancillary components—magazines, power generators, air-conditioning equipment, communications, storage, and service rooms—and often the fire-control plotting room as well, though in the case of many 16-inch installations the plotting room, because of firing concussion problems, occupied a separate underground site at some distance from the battery proper.

Because of the many new long-range batteries projected during this period, fire-control networks were greatly expanded. Although fire-direction radar instruments were introduced, the optical system was retained and a large number of new base-end stations were constructed. Some 16-inch batteries were provided with a dozen or more, and the distances between extreme sighting positions ran as high as fifty or sixty thousand yards. Along the flat Atlantic and Gulf coasts, the stations were generally located in towers; those on the Pacific were frequently dug in on elevated coastal slopes.

117. Inventories of seacoast artillery materiel, in RG 156, NA.

A notable exception to the general World War II style of fortifications occurred in Hawaii, where the threat of attack and invasion following the Pearl Harbor raid led to an emergency project that produced an extraordinary series of coastal batteries. Faced with a probable delay of a year or more in obtaining standard armament of the types prescribed under the general program, Army engineers took immediate advantage of the local availability of several heavy naval guns and turrets, some recovered from the sunken battleship *Arizona,* and others removed from the aircraft carriers *Lexington* and *Saratoga* during their modernization near the beginning of the war.[118]

The emplacement of this armament ashore was pushed on a round-the-clock schedule, and by the end of 1942 four excellent batteries, each comprising a pair of twin-gun 8-inch turrets, were ready for action (Figure 63). The various battery elements were entirely underground except for the armament, which was manned, supplied, and serviced from under as much as fifty feet of earth, rock, and concrete cover. A far more massive and complex pair of 14-inch batteries (see Figure 64), each to mount a single three-gun battleship turret, demanded appreciably greater construction time, and neither was ever fully completed.

The many obvious advantages of defensive works of this type marked the unique Hawaiian batteries as models of ideal coastal fortifications. Their cost was clearly prohibitive, however, and it was borne in this one instance only because no other solution to an acute need was possible under the prevailing circumstances of urgency, much as that of Fort Drum had been accepted three decades earlier in the absence of any technically feasible alternative.

The installation of new batteries under the World War II program proceeded rapidly during 1941 and for about a year after Pearl Harbor, as enemy gains in the Pacific brought the Japanese ultimately to positions on the Aleutian Islands. But as military and naval events in all theaters began to turn in favor of the Allies, the project was gradually curtailed until, about mid-1944, the shifting of the war away from American shores brought it essentially to a halt.[119]

118. The construction of these exceptional batteries is discussed in D. P. Kirchner and E. R. Lewis, "The Oahu Turrets," *The Military Engineer,* vol. 59, no. 392 (November-December 1967), pp. 430–433.

119. The program cutbacks were made in several stages, generally with Navy concurrence. See, for example, Conn, *Guarding the United States,* pp. 53–54; Letter, ACofS, OPD to Commander in Chief, U.S. Fleet, October 31, 1942, Subj: Seacoast Modernization Program (OPD 660.2 [9–21–42]), and Letter, Commander in Chief, United States Fleet and Chief of Naval Operations to CofS, U.S. Army, November 8, 1942, Subj: Modernization Program of Army Seacoast Defense Artillery (FF1/A16–3(4) Serial 001348); Letter, AGF to Chief of Engineers, SPRMS 660.2, 9 October 1943, based on Memo, OPD to CG, ASF, 5 October 1943 (OPD 660.2 [16 September 1943]).

FIGURE 59. A standard 16-inch battery of the World War II type. The casemate openings, 500 feet apart, were enclosed by 4-inch steel shields and protected by concrete canopies designed to absorb or deflect direct hits. The battery shown here was located on the Strait of Juan de Fuca, about 15 miles west of Port Angeles, Washington. Its field of fire covered not only the entrance to Puget Sound, but also the approaches to the harbor of Victoria, British Columbia, and the Canadian naval base at Esquimalt. Constructed between October 1942 and May 1945, this was the last of more than a dozen new 16-inch batteries to be completed in the continental United States during the war. Like many of the works finished late in the war, this battery was never named. (Photo, in author's collection, 1945)

FIGURE 60. A few hundred yards from the 16-inch battery shown in Figure 59 was this 6-inch battery, also unnamed, of typical World War II design. Nearly fifty batteries of this kind were built in the United States during the war, and about twenty more were constructed outside the continental limits. All were of similar plan, with the magazine complex between and slightly to the rear of the two guns, which were about 200 feet apart. Here can be seen the left gun of the battery and an entrance to the magazine beyond. The right gun is hidden by the slope under the tall trees. Unlike most of the World War II coastal armament, which dated from around 1920, the 6-inch carriage and its cast-steel shield were developed in 1940 and 1941. Some of the guns were also new, but many had originally been mounted on disappearing carriages, then on wheeled mounts for service in France during World War I. (Photo, in author's collection, 1945)

FIGURE 61. Similar in general arrangement to the 6-inch batteries, but about one-third again as large, were a very few 8-inch works constructed during World War II, all outside the continental United States. The guns were surplus Navy pieces transferred to the Army after the Washington Conference on the Limitation of Armaments, and the carriages were essentially the railway model of the 1930s less the railway car (see Figure 54). The first such battery was completed before the war near Little Compton, Rhode Island. With its guns casemated, it was basically a miniature version of the prototype 16-inch battery. Although additional 8-inch installations were originally to have been similarly casemated, the idea was dropped early in the war in favor of shields, to expedite the completion of serviceable batteries. Subsequently, the production order for shields was canceled, and the 8-inch guns, like this one overlooking Kaneohe Bay, Oahu, remained in the open, protected from above only by camouflage. (Photo SC-236046, U.S. Army Signal Corps, 1945)

A

B

C

D

FIGURE 62. The numerous battery installations of World War II were accompanied by the construction of a great many fire-control structures which, for major-caliber batteries, were situated along the coast for miles in either direction from the guns. These base-end stations took a variety of forms. An early type, which began to be used along the Atlantic coast long before World War II, was supported by an open steel framework and resembled a fire-lookout tower. Two stations of this kind (top, left) stood near San Juan, Puerto Rico, beside an SCR 296 seacoast artillery radar disguised as a water tower. Most of the stations built along the Atlantic during the war were simple closed concrete towers, either square or circular in plan. Two of several such towers are shown standing (top, right) near the mouth of the Delaware River. Some base-end stations were disguised as beachfront homes by false woodwork and even shingle roofs. Such a structure (lower left) may be seen on Point Judith, Rhode Island. Base-end stations along the Pacific coast, in Hawaii, and other areas where elevated sites were available near the ocean, were frequently dug in (lower right), with only the sighting aperture extended above ground level. (Photos: A, SC-380481, U.S. Army Signal Corps, 1943; B, by Colonel Riley McGarraugh, 1968; and C, by author, 1968. Drawing by author)

FIGURE 63. In the months following the Japanese attack on Pearl Harbor, most of the defensive armament installed in Hawaii consisted of surplus Navy guns, available at a time when distance and slow production made it impossible to obtain standard seacoast weapons. The majority were old deck guns of 3- to 5-inch caliber, mainly for beach defense against amphibious landings. In early 1942, however, a modernization of the aircraft carriers *Lexington* and *Saratoga,* which included the replacement of their original 8-inch cruiser-type armament with new 5-inch dual-purpose guns, made available for immediate use a total of eight turrets, each with a pair of long-range 8-inch guns. Army engineers designed and constructed four batteries of two turrets each in the remarkably short period of less than a year, despite their absolute lack of experience with fortification designs of this nature. Shown (left) under camouflage netting is one of the turrets of Battery Wilridge, named from its location on Wiliwilinui Ridge about four miles northeast of Diamond Head. (Photo, U.S. Army, 1943)

 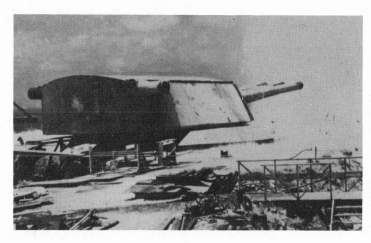

FIGURE 64. The heaviest naval armament available to the Army for installation in Hawaii consisted of the two rear turrets of the battleship *Arizona,* which had been sunk during the Pearl Harbor attack. Mounting three 14-inch guns each, these turrets were salvaged from the sunken ship during 1942, and most of the following year was spent in the reconditioning of the hundreds of mechanical and electrical components damaged during the raid and by subsequent immersion. A battery was commenced for each turret early in 1943. Like those for the 8-inch armament from the carriers (Figure 63), the battery structures, almost entirely underground, were designed to serve the armament from below. These single-turret batteries, located on opposite sides of Oahu, were named Arizona and Pennsylvania, the latter after the surviving sister of the ship from which the guns had come. Construction of Battery Arizona, on the island's west coast, was suspended short of completion, after the war. Battery Pennsylvania, sited at the tip of Mokapu Point to cover Kaneohe Bay and its approaches, and nearly completed when the war ended, is shown (right) during the proof firing of its three guns, four days before Japan's surrender and four days after the dropping of the first atomic bomb on Hiroshima. (Photo, U.S. Army, 1945)

Like most similar efforts before it, the World War II harbor defense program was not carried through to full realization. Many of its units were simply canceled, while construction of others was suspended pending a reappraisal of the program after the war. Of the more than 150 batteries projected, about two-thirds were brought to structural completion, but of these many were not provided with armament.[120]

Nevertheless, the program was anything but negligible, for between 1940 and 1945 it had consumed around one-quarter of a billion dollars and—even after the suspensions and cancellations—provided American harbors with the most extensive and formidably armed system of seacoast defenses in our history.[121]

After the surrender of Japan, certain of the batteries which had been deferred during the war were allowed to proceed to completion, the last of these being finished in 1948. By this time, however, most of the harbor defense facilities were in an inactive status and many had already been disposed of.[122] The technology of amphibious invasion, as demonstrated during World War II, had advanced to the point where large bodies of men and materiel could be landed under supporting air cover without the benefit of port facilities. Heavy ships' guns, if used at all, would be used in connection with such open-beach landings and not in bombarding coastal cities or naval bases, which could more safely and easily be attacked from the air. Thus, by 1948 the entire concept of harbor defense by long-range artillery stood on the verge of abandonment, an event that took place late that year and during 1949, when the last of the guns were scrapped. Not long afterward, at the beginning of 1950, the remaining harbor defense commands were disbanded, and the seacoast fortifications of the United States passed into history, leaving a rich assortment of stone, brick, and concrete monuments to the century and a half devoted to this form of defensive effort.[123]

A few months later the Coast Artillery was abolished as a separate branch of the Army and its units, entirely antiaircraft by this time, were recombined

120. Conn, *Guarding the United States*, p. 54; Memo, Logistics Group for ACofS, OPD, 24 October 1945 (OPD 660.2 [24 Oct 45]).

121. Memo (OPD 660.2 [24 Oct 45]).

122. See, for example, GO [General Order] 90, War Department, 15 August 1946; Circular 188, War Department, 19 July 1947; Circular 189, War Department, 22 July 1947; GO 77, War Department, 15 August 1947; Circular 23, Department of the Army, 16 October 1947.

123. Letter, The Adjutant General, Department of the Army, to Commanding Generals, First, Second, and Sixth Armies, 14 May 1948, Subj: Harbor Defense Installations (AGAO–S 660.2 [11 May 48], CSGSP/C 2); GO 1, Department of the Army, 3 January 1950.

with those of the Field Artillery into a single Artillery branch, in which many former Coast Artillery units retained their antiaircraft function and equipment.[124] In subsequent years the new antiaircraft guns and missiles, in many ways the functional descendants of the seacoast defenses, frequently continued to be manned by organizations that were the lineal descendants of the Coast Artillery Corps. In 1968 these once again attained separate status with the establishment of a new Air Defense Artillery branch.[125]

124. GO 23, Department of the Army, 20 July 1950; 64 Stat. 263 (June 28, 1950).
125. GO 25, Department of the Army, 14 June 1968; GO 37, Department of the Army, 12 June 1969.

Corregidor, September 1945

FIGURE 65. The centuries-old concept of harbor defense by fixed artillery was abandoned by most of the major nations during the ten years following World War II. In the United States, forts and batteries of secondary importance began to be phased out as early as 1946, and by 1949 the last of the guns at the major harbors such as Boston, New York, and San Francisco had been scrapped. The disposal of the armament was remarkably thorough. Few seacoast weapons were left in existence from the Endicott, Taft, World War I, or World War II periods. As a result, nineteenth-century smoothbores such as Rodman guns are today far more numerous despite their having been taken by the hundreds for the scrap drives of World War II. Nevertheless, a few post-1890 weapons survive, most of them on the island forts of Manila Bay, where they were battered first by the Japanese in 1942, then again by American bombers in 1945. Shown here as it appeared immediately after the war is a two-mortar pit of the Taft era, one of two such pits on Caballo Island. Many of the wrecked guns on Corregidor and its neighbor islands have since been grown over by jungle, but a few batteries are still maintained as memorials and tourist attractions. (Photo SC-225121, U.S. Army Signal Corps, 1945)

SEACOAST FORTIFICATIONS:

The Remnants and Their Prospects

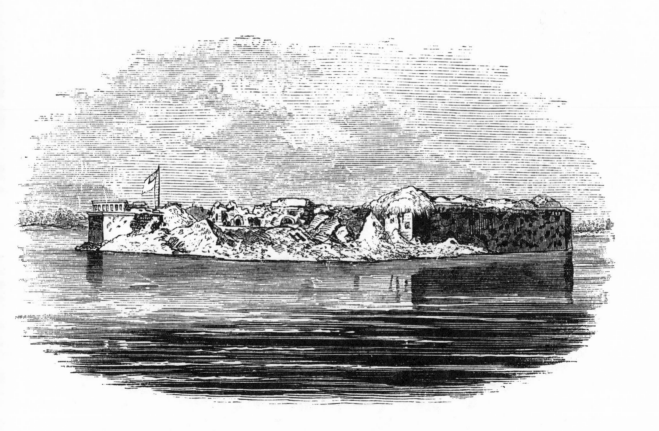

The Structures

From 1794 to the end of World War II, the harbor defense programs discussed in the preceding chapters produced between eight and nine hundred separate fortification structures, probably four-fifths of which are still in existence. The works of some periods have naturally survived in larger numbers than those of others because of the more durable materials of which they were built, the relative recency of their construction, and their status in terms of ownership since their abandonment for harbor defense purposes.

Other factors, of course, have played a part. For example, many works of the First and Second Systems (1794–1814) were demolished entirely to make way for later defenses, mainly in the course of Third System construction and during the Civil War but in a few instances as late as the Endicott period. Of the works still remaining from the first two periods, relatively few retain their original form, most having been reconstructed and modified between 1817 and 1865.

In general, earthworks have simply gone to pieces with the passage of time, though visible traces remain in certain localities, making it possible still to find occasional remnants of pre-1812 forts and of Third System detached batteries. The most numerous earthwork ruins, however, are those of batteries built during the early 1870s on tracts that are still in Army hands. These are frequently thought to be of a much earlier period, and in at least one case such a battery has been extensively repaired for presentation to the public as an example of a pre-Civil War defensive work.

The major forts of the Third System (1817–1867) have fared very well as a group. Despite the fact that some of them are badly in need of repair, practically all are still in existence, though a few have been modified markedly from their original form. The survival of this body of structures is of course due in part to the nature of their construction, but also to the fact that most of these works remained in service at least until World War I, while several served until World War II. Some, indeed, are still owned by the Army and continue to be maintained. Of the remainder, the majority are in state or municipal hands, while a few are under other federal agencies including the Navy and the Department of the Interior.

The Endicott period (1890–1910) produced more fortification structures than any other era, though a number have already been demolished, mainly in connection with nonmilitary construction such as highways, bridge anchorages, and approach roads. Hundreds are still in existence, however, on active Army posts, where the batteries are used for a variety of purposes, as well as on other federal lands or in state or city ownership, often on tracts maintained as park and recreation areas. In addition, a certain number are on privately owned property. The condition of Endicott period structures, as well as that of all later defenses, varies greatly. Some are badly deteriorated, while others appear to have been built within the last few years. Because their clean, functional design provides few clues as to their actual age, post-1890 seacoast defense works are often thought to be of much more recent origin than, in fact, they are; and casual visitors to an Endicott battery will almost invariably underestimate its age and judge it to date from World War I or even World War II. This apparent lack of antiquity may to some degree explain the general lack of interest in restoring such works for purely historical purposes.

Except for a half-dozen batteries at Fort MacArthur, near Los Angeles, all Taft period (1907–1920) construction was outside the continental United States, and practically every battery of this era remains intact, though the Manila Bay works, as already indicated, were badly damaged during World War II. Those in Hawaii and the Canal Zone, in contrast, tend to be in excellent condition, for most of the Taft period structures are still in military ownership and continue to be maintained.

The batteries built during and after World War I were few in number to begin with, and most were extensively modified after 1940 into the battery form of World War II, so that only a handful, for the most part outside the continental United States, remain as originally designed. The only good surviving specimens within the continental limits are two 12-inch gun batteries near Slaughter Beach, Delaware. Privately owned, their magazines have been converted to refrigeration plants and are used for the storage of pickles.

World War II batteries were constructed in substantial numbers, and few have been demolished. Many, still in Army, Navy, or Air Force hands, continue to be useful because of the massive overhead protection they offer for various ongoing military activities. A fair number are in state and private ownership. One or two of the larger works are being used as maximum security vaults for such things as corporation records, and at least two private homes have been built atop the magazine structures of 6-inch batteries.

In general, the six or seven hundred surviving fortification structures of all eras can be grouped into three categories: (1) those that simply continue to exist and deteriorate without maintenance; (2) those that are maintained, for one reason or another, to the extent of preventing further deterioration; and (3) those that have been or are being actively restored for historical purposes.

The first category is composed for the most part of Endicott period works that are badly deteriorated and in many cases unsafe for display to the public. Many stand on private property or within fenced off portions of public land, where maintenance is not required even for reasons of safety.

In the second category is the large number of structures located on still active military posts, where many are used as storage facilities or for other purposes, and in state or city owned parks or other recreation areas, where repairs are carried out primarily in the interests of public safety and only secondarily—if at all—for historical purposes. Historical efforts in connection with such works are usually limited to brief descriptive plaques or displays, which may or may not be accurate.

The third category comprises those relatively few works on which efforts have been or are being expended for reconstruction of great accuracy with the goal of historical restoration and preservation. Included for the most part are specimens of the Third System and earlier periods. Some of these, of course, were chosen because they were the scene of significant events (though later works of equal historical importance have been ignored); but it appears that restoration activities have focused on older defenses partly because of their comparative rarity and partly because they are more likely to be of interest to a public that tends to equate antiquity with historical and architectural value. The general neglect of Endicott and later works is undoubtedly due, at least in part, to the large numbers in which they survive, to their lack of resemblance to the traditional notion of forts, and to the fact, noted earlier, that their actual age is not readily apparent.

Restoration has been carried out to a limited extent by states, cities, and a few private organizations, and in view of the limited resources available for this purpose excellent results have occasionally been achieved. In the forefront of such activities, however, has been the United States Department of the Interior, whose resources include highly competent architects, historians, and archeologists. The Department's National Park Service presently administers several seacoast forts, including the colonial period Castillo de San Marcos, Fort McHenry of the First System, Castle Clinton of the Second, Fort Washington of the immediate post-1812 period, and Forts Sumter, Pulaski, and Jefferson of the Third System. Work is also in progress toward the restoration of an Endicott period battery of four 10-inch disappearing guns near Charleston, South Carolina.

The Weapons

Historical reconstruction of seacoast defenses has been, and increasingly will be hindered by the problem of obtaining suitable weapon specimens, for available seacoast smoothbores are rare, while post-1890 armament is virtually nonexistent.

Much of the pre-Civil War heavy ordnance, most of which was declared obsolete in the late 1860s, was disposed of around 1880, mainly through donations to individual cities and towns. Between about 1900 and 1910 most of the Civil War and post-Civil War seacoast armament, including more than a thousand Rodman guns, was similarly disposed of by donation, though some was sold for scrap. A great many of these old cannon remained for decades to decorate town squares and American Legion halls, but most of these appear to have been given up to a succession of scrap drives during World War II. In some instances, very rare pieces were donated to the war effort by citizens' groups, which had no basis for evaluation, while others of little historical value were retained. The number of nineteenth-century guns lost in this manner is indeterminate, but it is almost certain that the percentage held back was small. And while these, for the most part, are still in existence, many are on courthouse lawns a thousand miles from the sea, and the reluctance of town councils to surrender them is understandable.

Armament of the Endicott and later periods is much rarer still. A considerable number of 3-, 4-, 4.7-, 5-, and 8-inch guns were classed as obsolete in 1920 and, like the smoothbores, many were donated to communities and to veterans' groups, but few survived the scrap drives of World War II. The metals requirements of that war also claimed the remaining Endicott and Taft period armament almost without exception, for as new post-1940 batteries neared completion, nearby disappearing guns and mortars were inactivated and cut up with torches within their emplacements. As noted in the preceding chapter, the destruction of World War II armament in 1948 and 1949 was also virtually complete, leaving fewer than a dozen pieces that seem to have escaped scrapping almost through oversight.

A very few states have been exceptionally fortunate in securing post-1890 seacoast armament, for the most part prior to World War II. Florida's Fort DeSoto Park near Tampa, for example, is a former Endicott period installation that was abandoned by the Army around 1930 with the 12-inch mortars still in place. For its parks at Forts Flagler and Casey, the state of Washington was recently able to obtain a half-dozen pieces, including two 10-inch disappearing guns, from the body of weapons remaining in the Philippines after World War II, but these were about the only weapons of that collection still in a condition for use as display items. In this regard, Washington was fortunate in having moved early to secure them, for it is doubtful if any of the other guns or mortars on Corregidor or its neighbor forts would be useful even if they were now to be made available, a possibility hardly worth considering.

As a result of this general shortage of seacoast armament and a heightened interest during recent years in the American military heritage, it has been necessary to resort to the production of smoothbore replicas, many of which are on display at various forts, parks, and battlefields (see Figure 32). So far as is known, there have not yet been any attempts to reproduce post-1890 seacoast armament in full scale, but this will eventually have to be done if any Endicott or later batteries are to be completely restored. Because of the size and complexity of such weapons, the making of replicas will undoubtedly be a very involved and expensive affair.

It is to be hoped that at least a few of the later batteries will nevertheless be restored to include armament facsimiles. Devoid of guns, most of these —unlike the older works—provide few other clues as to their function in the history of American defense. As a result, the occasional visitor is often left with no idea of what they are, when they were built, or what they were used for.

POSTSCRIPT

By Harold L. Peterson, *Chief Curator, National Park Service*

From its birth the new United States placed itself among the foremost of those countries which considered seacoast protection a prime necessity. The great forts that it built, with their emphasis on defense rather than aggression, reflected the American attitude in an age that hoped for a peaceful aloofness from the rest of the world yet determined to defend itself from any possible foreign attack. The skill of American engineers translated these hopes into one of the most advanced coastal defense systems in the world. For 150 years their creations guarded the nation's borders on all three coasts, as well as the detached territories.

But all eras must end. In 1903 Orville and Wilbur Wright gave notice that the sea was no longer the only approach to America. Soon carrier-based aircraft demonstrated that the best fort could be bypassed. Still, the coastal fort survived and added antiaircraft weapons to its armament. Then in 1944 Germany launched its first V-1 rocket against England. It was crude, but its intercontinental successors made the seacoast fort obsolete almost overnight. They closed the era that cannon began.

Today, the coastal fort is a relic. The impressive walls of earth or stone, of brick or reinforced concrete are no longer important from a military standpoint. The missile silo has usurped a function long held by larger and frequently more esthetic structures. Vulnerability to attack is now spread throughout a nation, and the narrow strip along the verge of the sea has lost its defensive significance. The structures built to guard it have become peaceful tourist attractions.

The National Park Service administers ten areas which contain noteworthy examples of the coastal fortifications of the United States from the First System through the disappearing-gun batteries of the Endicott period and even a few remnants of later defenses. Each year these historic structures are visited by hundreds of thousands of Americans from all walks of life, while additional multitudes find their way to coastal forts preserved by state and local agencies. Some of these visitors seek merely a diversion from daily routine; others are interested in American history in general; and still others are students of architecture, of engineering, or of military science. No matter what their motivation, all are visibly impressed by the engineering skill and the craftsmanship involved in creating the big masonry forts, and the great majority seemingly also come away with a feeling of history, a sense of having made contact with a tangible substance of the past, a shadow of another era.

FIGURE 66. On the night of June 21, 1942, Battery David Russell at Fort Stevens, Oregon, came under fire from a Japanese submarine that had surfaced off the mouth of the Columbia River. It thus became the only seacoast fortification in the continental United States to be fired upon by an enemy naval vessel of a foreign power since the War of 1812. In virtually every other respect, Battery Russell typifies hundreds of existing post-1890 works, not only in its design, which makes it an excellent example of the Endicott period, but also in its present condition. Begun in 1903, the two-gun 10-inch battery remained in service for nearly forty years, until well into World War II. Since 1947, when the defenses of the Columbia were discontinued, the battery structure has been allowed to deteriorate, and although its eventual restoration by the state of Oregon is planned, the concrete continues to chip and crumble. As with most batteries accessible to the public, many of the iron fittings such as railings and ladders have suffered severe rusting and have been replaced for reasons of safety, while the large expanses of concrete have provided irresistible canvases for one of the leading national forms of public expression. (Photos by Marshall Hanft, 1958 and 1969)

SELECTED BIBLIOGRAPHY

The documentary sources used in the preparation of this account of American seacoast fortifications consist for the most part of unpublished records, many of which have been cited in the footnotes, where record group designations have been provided to indicate their locations in the National Archives or in various record depositories of the Department of the Army.

Of the published materials used, many are not ordinarily available except at a few libraries such as the Library of Congress and the Army Library at the Pentagon. This bibliography, therefore, is restricted to works that deal with the subject in more than a passing or peripheral manner, and that should be available in any large community or university library.

Abbot, Henry L. *Course of Lectures Upon the Defence of the Sea-Coast of the United States.* New York: D. Van Nostrand, 1888.

American State Papers, Military Affairs. 7 vols. Washington: Gales and Seaton, 1832–1861.

Arthur, Robert. *History of Fort Monroe.* Fort Monroe, Virginia: The Coast Artillery School, 1930.

———. "Coast Forts in Colonial New Hampshire." *The Coast Artillery Journal,* vol. 58, no. 6 (June 1923), pp. 547–553.

———. "Coast Forts of Colonial Massachusetts." *The Coast Artillery Journal,* vol. 58, no. 2 (February 1923), pp. 101–122.

———. "Coast Forts of Colonial New Jersey, Pennsylvania, and Delaware." *The Coast Artillery Journal,* vol. 69, no. 1 (July 1928), pp. 46–59.

———. "Colonial Coast Forts on the South Atlantic." *The Coast Artillery Journal,* vol. 70, no. 1 (January 1929), pp. 41–62.

Barnes, Frank. *Fort Sumter National Monument, South Carolina.* National Park Service Historical Handbook Series Number 12. Washington: Government Printing Office, 1952.

Belote, James H. and William M. *Corregidor: The Saga of a Fortress.* New York: Harper & Row, 1967.

Birkhimer, William E. *Historical Sketch of the Organization, Administration, Matériel and Tactics of the Artillery, United States Army.* Washington: Chapman, 1884.

Bruff, Lawrence L. *A Text-Book of Ordnance and Gunnery Prepared for the Use of Cadets of the U.S. Military Academy.* New York: John Wiley & Sons, 1896.

Chief of Engineers, United States Army. Annual Reports, 1866–1910.

Conn, Stetson; Engelman, Rose C.; and Fairchild, Byron. *Guarding the United States and Its Outposts.* Volume in United States Army in World War II: The Western Hemisphere. Washington: Department of the Army, 1964.

Crowell, Benedict. *America's Munitions*. Washington: Government Printing Office, 1919.

————, and Wilson, Robert Forrest. *The Armies of Industry*. Vol. 1. New Haven: Yale University Press, 1921.

Falk, Stanley L. "Artillery for the Land Service: The Development of a System." *Military Affairs,* vol. 28, no. 3 (Fall 1964), pp. 97–110.

Gibbon, John. *The Artillerist's Manual*. New York: D. Van Nostrand, 1860.

Griffin, Eugene. *Our Sea-Coast Defences*. The Military Service Institution: Military Monographs No. 1. New York: G. P. Putnam's Sons, 1885.

Halleck, H[enry] Wager. *Elements of Military Art and Science; or, Course of Instruction in Strategy, Fortification, Tactics of Battles, &c.* New York: D. Appleton & Co., 1846.

Holley, Alexander L. *A Treatise on Ordnance and Armor*. New York: Trubner & Co., 1865.

Kirchner, D. P., and Lewis, E. R. "American Harbor Defenses: The Final Era." *United States Naval Institute Proceedings,* vol. 94, no. 1 (January 1968), pp. 84–98.

————. "The Oahu Turrets." *The Military Engineer,* vol. 59, no. 392 (November-December 1967), pp. 430–433.

Lattimore, Ralston B. *Fort Pulaski National Monument, Georgia*. National Park Service Historical Handbook Series Number 18. Washington: Government Printing Office, 1954.

Lewis, Emanuel R. "The Ambiguous Columbiads." *Military Affairs,* vol. 28, no. 3 (Fall 1964), pp. 111–122.

Manucy, Albert C. *The Building of Castillo de San Marcos*. National Park Service Interpretive Series, History Number 1. Washington: Government Printing Office, n.d. [reprinted 1961].

Morton, Louis. *The Fall of the Philippines*. Volume in United States Army in World War II: The War in the Pacific. Washington: Department of the Army, 1953.

Ordnance Department, United States Army. *A Collection of Annual Reports and Other Important Papers Relating to the Ordnance Department.* 4 vols. Washington: Government Printing Office, 1878–1890.

Totten, J. G. *Report of the Chief Engineer on the Subject of National Defences*. Washington: A. Boyd Hamilton, 1851.

U.S. Congress. House. *Report of the Board on Fortifications or Other Defenses Appointed by the President of the United States Under the Provisions of the Act of Congress Approved March 3, 1885*. H. Exec. Doc. 49, 49th Cong., 1st Sess., 1886.

————. Senate. *Report on the Means of National Defence*. In S. Exec. Doc. 85, 28th Cong., 2d Sess., 1845.

————. Senate. *Coast Defenses of the United States and the Insular Possessions*. S. Doc. 248, 59th Cong., 1st Sess., 1906.

APPENDIX

A—*Positions Fortified Under Various Harbor Defense Programs*

With the exceptions noted below, the following table lists every locality fortified under one or more of the programs discussed in the text. In certain instances (e.g., Newport and Narragansett Bay, Rhode Island), more than one position is shown for the same general area, reflecting the outward shifting of defensive works due to technological advances (see pages 9–13 of the text). The defended harbors and rivers are arranged by states, except where the waterways themselves lay between states and were protected by defenses sited in two or even three states (e.g., Long Island Sound was guarded by forts in New York, Connecticut, and Rhode Island, and the Delaware, Potomac, and Columbia Rivers were similarly defended by forts in more than one state).

Not included in this tabulation are the following classes of defenses:

1. Fortifications proposed under one or more programs but never constructed;

2. Fortifications begun between the end of the Civil War and 1875, the majority of which were not completed;

3. Fortifications of a temporary nature, constructed usually but not invariably during wartime, which were not part of a permanent program; or

4. Fortifications on the Great Lakes or elsewhere along the northern frontier, some of which (aside from location) were basically of the types described in the text.

Each of the positions listed in the table is followed by one or more of the symbols shown immediately below to indicate the programs under which it was fortified. The numbers in parentheses after place names indicate the figures in the text illustrating works or weapons at these locations.

Symbol   *Indicates positions at which*—

1   Fortifications were constructed during the years 1794-1804.

2   Fortifications were constructed during the years 1807-1814.

3   Permanent fortifications were constructed at any time between 1817 and 1867, either original works or retained, restored, and/or modified older American or Spanish types.

E   Fortifications were constructed between 1890 and 1910 under the program initiated by the Endicott Board.

T   The first fortification by the United States took place between 1907 and 1920 as a result of the recommendations of the Taft Board.

I   Long-range 12- or 16-inch armament was installed following World War I and prior to 1936.

R   Railway artillery was provided at any time between 1919 and 1943.

II   Fortifications were constructed between 1937 and 1945.

Location	Program				Location	Program			
Maine:					**Connecticut:**				
Passamaquoddy Bay	2				New London	1 2 3			
Machias	2				New Haven	2			
Penobscot River	2 3				Long Island Sound	aE	I	II	
St. George's River	2								
Damariscotta River	2				**New York:**				
Sheepscot River	2				Sag Harbor	2			
Kennebec River	2 3 E				New York (front endpaper, 7, 9-12, 23, 29, 47)	1 2 3 E	I R II		
Portland (26)	1 2 3 E	I	II						
New Hampshire:					Delaware River (2, 5, 62B)	1 2 3 E	I R II		
Portsmouth	1 2 3 E	II							
Massachusetts:					**Maryland:**				
Newburyport	2				Baltimore (4,6,27)	1 2 3 E			
Gloucester	1 2				Annapolis	b1 2 3			
Salem	1 2								
Marblehead	1 2				Potomac River (32, 34, 46)	2 3 E			
Boston (14, 44)	1 2 3 E	I	II						
Plymouth	2				**Virginia:**				
New Bedford	2 3 E	I	II		Alexandria	b1			
Rhode Island:					James River	2			
Newport (22)	1 2 3				Norfolk (8)	1 2			
Narragansett Bay (62C)	E	II							

Location	Program
Hampton Roads (15, 17, 21, 41, 43)	3 E
Chesapeake Bay	I R II
North Carolina:	
Ocracoke Inlet	b1
Beaufort	2 3
Cape Fear River	1 2 3 E
South Carolina:	
Georgetown	b1 2
Charleston (25, 31, 45)	1 2 3 E II
Beaufort	2
Port Royal Sound	aE
Georgia:	
Savannah (16, 24, 33)	1 2 3 E
St. Mary's River	1 2
Cumberland Sound	3
Florida:	
St. Augustine (3)	3
Key West (40, back endpaper)	3 E II
Dry Tortugas (28)	3
Tampa	aE
Pensacola	3 E I II

Location	Program
Alabama:	
Mobile	3 E
Mississippi:	
Mississippi Sound	3
Louisiana:	
Passes between Lake Borgne and Lake Pontchartrain	3
Bayou Bienvenue	3
New Orleans	2
Mississippi River	2 3 E
Barataria Bay	3
Texas:	
Galveston	E I II
California:	
San Diego	E II
Los Angeles	cT R II
San Francisco (19, 30, 35, 36, 38, 55, 58)	3 E I II
Columbia River (37, 66)	E R II
Washington:	
Puget Sound (59, 60)	aE R II

Location	Program
Philippine Islands:	
Manila Bay (48, 49, 65)	T I R
Subic Bay	T
Hawaii, Oahu (50):	R
Honolulu (63)	T II
Pearl Harbor (39, 56)	T I II
Kaneohe Bay (61, 64)	II
North Shore, Oahu	II
Panama Canal Zone:	R
Balboa (Pacific end) (52B, 57)	T I II
Cristobal (Atlantic end)	T I II
Cuba:	
Guantanamo	dT

Location	Program
Alaska:	
Sitka	II
Seward	II
Kodiak	II
Dutch Harbor	II
Puerto Rico:	
San Juan (62A)	II
Vieques Sound (Roosevelt Roads)	II
Newfoundland:	
Argentia and St. Johns	R II
Bermuda:	R II
Trinidad:	II

a Long Island Sound, Port Royal Sound; Tampa, and Puget Sound, though not listed in the report of the Endicott Board, were added in the 1890's to the project initiated by that body.

b The First System works at Annapolis, Alexandria, Ocracoke, and Georgetown were begun but never completed.

c Los Angeles, though unlisted by the Taft Board, was added in 1908.

d Batteries were constructed at Guantanamo, but their armament was not installed, being held in reserve at an arsenal. The weapons were eventually transferred to the United States Marine Corps.

B — Characteristics of Principal Seacoast Weapons, 1794-1945

This tabulation presents certain characteristics of seacoast weapons which have been selected to represent the various periods discussed in the text. Only a few of the many models of armament have been listed, but the principal piece of each period (major-caliber) has been included to permit comparisons of maximum power and coverage capabilities.

Weapon, Caliber, and Type [1]	Weight (lb.)		Maximum Range			Muzzle Velocity (fps)	Cost [5] (Gun & Carr.)
	Gun [2]	Projectile	Yards	Miles Approx.	At Elev. (Deg.) [4]		
1794–1814 (First and Second Systems)							
24-pdr SB	5,500	24	[3]	(1)	5	[3]	700
32-pdr SB	7,500	32	1,920	(1)	5	1640	800
1817–1867 (Third System)							
42-pdr SB	8,500	42	1,960	(1)	5	1640	900
10-inch SB	15,400	125	5,660	(3)	39	1250	1,600
1860–1890							
15-inch SB [6]	49,100	315	5,020	(3)	30	1300	9,000
	49,100	434	7,730	(4)	32	1510	10,500
1890–1910 Endicott Period							
12-inch RG	116,000	1070	13,500	(8)	10	2250	90,000
12-inch RM	29,000	700	15,200	(9)	45	1500	23,000
6-inch RG	19,000	108	16,000	(9)	15	2600	21,000
1907–1920 Taft Period							
14-inch RG	138,000	1560	24,000	(14)	20	2370	165,000
12-inch RM	33,000	700	19,300	(11)	45	1850	24,000
1917–1936							
16-inch RG (Army)	385,000	2340	49,100	(28)	53	2700	600,000
12-inch RG	118,000	975	30,100	(17)	35	2350	145,000
1937–1945							
16-inch RG (Navy)	307,000	2240	45,100	(26)	47	2750	750,000
6-inch RG	22,000	105	27,000	(15)	47	2800	120,000
Railway Artillery							
14-inch RG	234,000	1400	48,200	(27)	48	3000	430,000
8-inch RG [7]	33,000	260	24,900	(14)	42	2600	80,000
	42,000	260	35,300	(20)	45	2840	110,000

1. In this column, SB—smoothbore; RG and RM—rifled gun and mortar, respectively.

2. Less carriage. For various patterns between 1794 and 1840, average weights are given.

3. For early 24-pounders ranges and muzzle velocities varied, but were generally of the order of one mile and 1300-1600 feet per second.

4. Where maximum range was attained at less than 45°, elevation was restricted by carriage design.

5. Costs varied considerably, both with the date and from manufacturer to manufacturer. The figures given are, in most instances, rough averages. Those for the first two periods are estimates only; costs were neither fixed nor published.

6. Upper figures are for Civil War period, lower, for period around 1880, when a heavier propelling charge and a stronger carriage were used.

7. Upper figures are for World War I model, lower for model of late 1930s.

INDEX

Illustrations are indicated by numbers in italics